Communion
with
Our God

Communion
with
Our God

Paula Rodriguez

Tanglewood Publishing

Communion with Our God

By Paula Rodriguez

Copyright 2012 by Tanglewood Publishing

ISBN-13: 978-0-9793718-9-9
ISBN-10: 0-9793718-9-9

Tanglewood Publishing
Clinton, Mississippi
800-241-4016

Cover Photo from istockphoto.com

Cover Layout and Design by Sara Renick/Indigenous Images

Book design and layout by Martha Nichols/aMuse Productions®

Printed in the United States of America

VERY SPECIAL THANKS

AS WITH THE FIRST TWO BOOKS IN THIS SERIES, I WANT TO THANK MY editor for this project, Amy Carter. I first met Amy when she was twelve or thirteen years old, and I was a friend of her mother. Amy has since earned a master's degree in English and is now a friend in her own right. She has been through every lesson, and has not only answered all of the questions, but edited all of the written work. Amy, I will forever be grateful for your help with this project.

For theological guidance, I once again turned to some of my many pastor friends. Each one gave me valuable advice and encouragement. I would like to thank my husband, Charlie Rodriguez, and also Ken Elliott, Matt Giesman, Simon Kistemaker, Alan Kolodny, Paul Lipe, Don Malin, Elias Medeiros, John Reeves, and Guy Waters for helping me to make sure the comments in this study are theologically valid and in accordance with Scripture and the Westminster Standards.

TABLE OF CONTENTS

INTRODUCTION

THE *WESTMINSTER CONFESSION OF FAITH* AND THE SHORTER CATECHISM which grew out of it are statements of doctrine, of what many people believe are the teachings of the Bible. We who were involved in writing this study believe that they contain the best summary of what God has revealed to us through His Word. We also believe that if a person understands these teachings, they will bring much peace and comfort to his or her life in Christ. But we do not believe that understanding all of this doctrine is necessary to salvation.

The truths contained in the Shorter Catechism cannot be understood unless a person first has come to a saving knowledge of Jesus Christ. These truths are spiritually understood; they do not make sense to the human mind without the guidance of the Holy Spirit. If you have not yet established a personal relationship with Jesus Christ, this might not be the right time for this study. If you choose to continue with it, please remember that salvation comes first, then very slowly, the understanding of the knowledge of God. This particular study considers the Ten Commandments. Although these commands are from God, and are still important for our daily lives, we cannot be saved simply by obeying these laws.

Neither is The Shorter Catechism or the *Westminster Confession of Faith* the gospel. The Gospel is very simple: "Believe in the Lord Jesus Christ, and you will be saved." This means that we must understand that we are sinners and have broken the law of God, and that therefore we deserve to be punished. But Christ, in His mercy, took on our sins and died in our place. If we accept His death as punishment for our sins and agree to live in obedience to Him, out of our love and gratitude to Him, we will live forever with Him in eternity. That is the Gospel. The Shorter Catechism seeks to teach believers the doctrine of what we call the Reformed faith.

That is where this study comes in. Our goal is that by entering into this study, you will gain a better understanding of some of the basics of our faith as they are explained in the *Westminster Confession of Faith* and the Larger and Shorter Catechisms.

There are some parts of the Shorter Catechism that are easy to understand and others that are very difficult. God leads each of us into understanding of this doctrine in our own time; so if there are things that seem too hard to take in, we encourage you to pray, search the Scripture, and then let God lead you in your own time as He directs. We also encourage you to be patient with others as they take their own individual journey through the mysteries of God's plan. Let God be God. He is much better at it than we are.

THE WESTMINSTER CONFESSION AND CATECHISMS

ON MAY 13, 1643, THE BRITISH PARLIAMENT ORGANIZED AN ASSEMBLY of ministers (or "divines") to create standards for a Church of England that would be reformed in worship, government, and doctrine. The Assembly comprised 151 members, including 30 laymen, chosen by Parliament to represent the counties, the universities, the House of Lords, and the House of Commons. Three were ministers of the Reformed Church of France, serving congregations in Canterbury and London. Twenty-eight did not attend, and twenty-one were appointed later to replace members who did not attend or who died during the proceedings.

The Westminster divines, mostly teachers and pastors of churches, were described by the Parliament as "learned, godly, and judicious." And they were. The Assembly's members were all Calvinists in theology; the main difference among them was in their views of church government and discipline. This resulted in a number of groups or parties—moderate Episcopalians (most of whom declined to attend out of loyalty to the king), Presbyterians (much the largest group), and Congregationalists.

The Assembly met at first in Westminster Abbey's imposing Henry VII Chapel. As the weather turned cooler, the divines were glad to move to the more comfortable Jerusalem Chamber. Every member took a vow to "maintain nothing in point of doctrine but what I believe to be most agreeable to the Word of God; nor in point of discipline, but what may make most for God's glory and the peace and good of his Church." The Assembly met every day except Saturday and Sunday, from nine o'clock until one or two. In the afternoons, the divines worked in committees. One of the rules guiding the deliberations required that "what any man undertakes to prove as necessary, he shall make good out of Scripture." The minutes and other reports of the Assembly's work reveal a strong commitment to this rule.

Much of the time of the Westminster divines was taken up with preaching and hearing sermons. Many hours were spent in corporate prayer and discussion concerning the lessons of God's providence. There were 1,163 numbered sessions of the Westminster Assembly, the last coming on February 22, 1649.

Over the course of five and a half years, during a time of political and religious chaos, the Westminster Assembly created five great documents of theological orthodoxy and ecclesiastical stability for the church in England, Ireland, and Scotland.

The *Westminster Confession of Faith* is the Assembly's most important work. Drawing on the richness of the creeds and confessions of church history, the Westminster divines summed up in thirty-three chapters "what man is to believe concerning God, and what duty God requires of man." The Westminster Assembly also produced two catechisms—"one more exact and comprehensive, another more easy and short for new beginners." The Larger Catechism was completed in October 1647 and The Shorter Catechism a month later.

The Westminster Confession has been translated into many languages and has shaped Reformed churches and thought throughout the world. Its biblical faithfulness has helped many to know "how we may glorify and enjoy" God.

—Excerpted from David B. Calhoun, "The Westminster Assembly." *The Confessions of Our Faith*. The Fortress Edition. 2007. Used with permission.

A NOTE TO WOMEN

WHY DOES A WOMAN NEED TO KNOW ABOUT THE SHORTER CATECHISM? Shouldn't we leave the doctrine up to the men of the church? Well, that depends on what you mean by doctrine and how you want it taught.

If by doctrine you mean the decisions about the official statements as to what a particular denomination believes, then, yes, many denominations believe that the Bible teaches that those decisions should be left up to the men. But there are denominations that include women in making those decisions. And although the *Westminster Confession of Faith* addresses this issue, the Shorter Catechism does not, so we will not address it in this discussion either. However, if by doctrine you mean the things we need to know and understand about God and Jesus Christ, then aren't these the things that we talk to our friends, family, and children about on a daily basis? I hope so. And how sad if our only answer to the questions of others is, "I don't know. You'll have to ask a man."

We certainly believe that women are intelligent enough to handle Biblical doctrine, and we think God believes so too. There are plenty of examples in the Bible to indicate this. Timothy was reminded by Paul to continue in the teaching he received from his mother and grandmother. Priscilla and Aquila are mentioned together; they worked hand-in-hand in spreading the Gospel. Many other women are commended by Paul in his letters to other Christians.

So let's not for a minute think that we don't have a place in doctrine. As I was writing this, I began to wonder why, if women are so instrumental in teaching doctrine to others, are most of the commands to teach our children given to men? Of course, God has given the ultimate responsibility for the household to the husband and father. But also, because it comes naturally to women to teach their children, there is no need for God to command us to do so. Proverbs 1:8 admonishes, "Hear, my son, your father's instruction, and forsake not your mother's teaching." It is just assumed that mothers will teach their children. But we do need to be certain that we are doing it right. That is the purpose of this study.

HOW TO USE THIS STUDY

AS A TEACHER, I ALWAYS WANT MY STUDENTS TO BE PREPARED WHEN they come to class. I want them to be familiar with the material before they hear what I have to say about it.

That is the way I have approached this study. First, I want you to be familiar with the material. I want you to see for yourself what Scripture has to say about these doctrines. I have done that by giving you questions to answer related to each of the Catechism questions. After you have answered the questions, then read what I have to say. Test what I say against what you have read. Your discussions will be much richer if you have prepared each lesson.

Finally, many people like to memorize the Catechism questions and answers. That is not my purpose, but I am not opposed to it. It is much more important, however, to understand the truths of the words than to memorize the words themselves.

The Shorter Catechism questions and answers used in this study are from the Fortress Edition, which is a standard English edition. This edition seeks to maintain the original wording of the Confession and Catechisms as often as possible, while updating archaic or obsolete language to make it more understandable to the modern reader.

If you have questions about the doctrines contained in these studies, please ask your pastor about them. I would also be happy to discuss these things with you via email. My address is paula.catechism@gmail.com.

1

LESSON 1
A SIN IS STILL A SIN

Question 82: Is any man able to keep perfectly the commandments of God?

Answer: No mere man, since the Fall, is able, in this life, to keep perfectly the commandments of God, but does break them daily, in thought, word, and deed.

1. What does God require us to do?
    Read 1 Kings 8:61; 1 John 2:3

2. Does anyone do this?
    Read Ecclesiastes 7:20; Romans 3:12

3. If we fail to obey God's commands, what does this mean for us?
    Read Romans 3:10; Psalm 143:2

4. What are we doing to ourselves and to God if we claim that we have not sinned?
    Read 1 John 1:8, 10

Question 83: Are all transgressions of the law equally wicked?

Answer: Some sins in themselves, and by reason of aggravating circumstances, are more wicked in the sight of God than others.

5. Under Old Testament law, what was the penalty for murder or kidnapping?
    Read Exodus 21:12-16

6. Under Old Testament law, what was the penalty for theft?
    Read Exodus 22:1-3

Question 84: What does every sin deserve?

Answer: Every sin deserves God's wrath and curse, both in this life and that which is to come.

7. What was the first sin?
    Read Genesis 3:6

8. How was Eve tempted to eat the fruit?
    Read Genesis 3:5

9. What are the reasons for the wrath of God?
    Read Micah 7:9; Romans 2:8; Ephesians 2:3

10. What are the reasons for the curse of God?
    Read Deuteronomy 11:26-28; Malachi 2:2; Galatians 3:10

11. Why can we not be trusted to know what is right and wrong?
    Read Proverbs 12:15, 14:12, 21:2

LESSON 1
A SIN IS STILL A SIN

Catechism Questions 82, 83, and 84

CAN YOU THINK OF ANYTHING YOU HAVE EVER DONE WRONG? I HOPE you think that is a ridiculous question. My list would take pages and pages. How about yours? Of course, we all do things we shouldn't or don't do things we should. That's just human nature, right? Well, sort of. It's not human nature, it's our human sin nature. The first humans didn't have that nature. They were able to live totally without sin, at least for a while. But then they chose to do the one thing they were not supposed to do, and from that point on we have all inherited that sinfulness.

The problem is that God's law requires that we keep it perfectly, that we never, ever do anything we are not supposed to do or fail to do anything we are supposed to do. Let's review the Ten Commandments, the summary of the Law of God. I am including my own short explanation of each commandment for clarification.

1. You shall have no other gods before me. [You shall not give anything other than God first priority in your life.]

2. You shall not make for yourselves a carved image. You shall not bow down to them or serve them. [You shall not use a representation of God as an aid to worship or worship anything man-made.]

3. You shall not take the name of the Lord your God in vain. [You shall always speak of God and all His attributes and all His works in an honorable way.]

4. Remember the Sabbath day to keep it holy. [Do all your work in six days, and rest and honor the Lord on the seventh day.]

5. Honor your father and your mother. [Respect your parents, speak well of them, and provide for them in their need.]

6. You shall not murder. [Do not take the life of an innocent person or wish ill on anyone.]

7. You shall not commit adultery. [Do not have sex outside of marriage or use impure language or have impure thoughts.]

8. You shall not steal. [Do not take anything that does not belong to you, including ideas, and give to the Lord what He is due.]

9. You shall not bear false witness against your neighbor. [Do not lie to one another, especially to cause trouble for an innocent person or to make yourself look better.]

10. You shall not covet. [Do not want anything that someone else has.]

In reviewing that list, can you find one or two of those commandments that you have broken? If you have broken even one of them, one time, you have not kept God's law perfectly. And we know that we have all broken more than one, many more times than once. So we are faced with the wrath of God, which we will get to in a bit.

You have probably heard that all sins are equal in the sight of God, and in one sense that is true. But in another sense it is not. Even when He was giving the specific laws for the punishment of criminals, God did not order the same punishment for every crime. Taking a life is not the same as stealing an object, and God did not treat those crimes the same. We instinctively know that. Even criminals know that. Even in prison, those who have committed crimes against children are subject to much more cruel treatment from other prisoners than those who have broken other laws.

So why are we told that all sins are the same? Because in another sense, they are the same. The first sin ever recorded doesn't really seem so bad; Adam and Eve ate something they weren't supposed to eat. They didn't kill anyone; they didn't even take something that didn't belong to them. They just ate fruit that they were told not to eat. As a result of that sin, they were thrown out of the Garden of Eden and made to work hard for the rest of their lives. At first glance, it doesn't seem like the punishment fit the crime.

But what really was the crime? It was much more than eating the fruit. It was wanting to be like God. It was actually wanting to be their own god, to make their own rules. When they ate that fruit, they were saying to God, "We don't care what your rules are; we will do what we want to do. We will be our own gods and we will make our own rules." And the punishment fits that crime very well.

Whenever we sin, that is exactly what we are saying to God. We are saying that we are going to be our own god and make our own rules. We are going to feel free to disobey God's rules and obey our own. Have you ever heard a child say to another child, "You're not the boss of me"? Well, that is exactly what we are saying to God every time we fail to do what we know is right.

In that sense, every sin is the same. Every sin is rebellion against God, or wanting to be our own god. Every sin involves our saying to God, "I will take charge of my life now and follow my own rules. I am not interested in following your rules because you are not the boss of me. I am my own god." We create rules which please us, following them when it suits us and forgiving ourselves when we don't. We act in every way as gods. But there are big problems with this scenario.

The first problem is that we can't be trusted to know what is best because we are very foolish people. We make decisions on little knowledge, on what seems good at the moment. But God has all knowledge. He knows all of the potential consequences for all of our actions, and He knows how our actions can affect others.

Have you ever been in the car with someone who is obviously lost but absolutely will not stop to ask for directions? I will not mention a specific gender of person who often does this, but I'll bet you can guess. These people will tell you that they know what they're doing, that they will get there pretty soon, that the road signs are all messed up, anything but admit that they are hopelessly lost. Meanwhile, everyone else in the car has to suffer along until they give up or miraculously stumble on the right road. That's a pretty good picture of how we run our own lives. We think we know what we're doing, but we can get everything all turned around and get ourselves hopelessly lost. And everyone else in our lives has to suffer along with us until we get things right. The way that seems right to us can be the road that ends in death. God not only knows the way, He *is* the way. If we will follow His direction, we will always be on the right road.

The second problem is that we are not gods. We are created beings acting in rebellion against the One True God. And in our rebellion, we deserve God's wrath and curse. We break the first commandment by setting ourselves up as our own gods, and then proceed to keep or discard each of the other nine commandments as we see fit. But God does not give us that privilege. He demands obedience. By breaking His law, we actually put ourselves under His wrath and curse.

Did you ever watch "The Cosby Show"? Bill Cosby played a father of five children, and one of his most famous lines from that program was, "I'm your father. I brought you into this world, and I can take you out." All parents can identify with that line. We wouldn't really take out our children, but we understand the feeling. And fathers don't really bring their children into the world, either. They contribute half of the genetic material, but all human beings are created by God. So it is God who brings us into the world, and it is God who takes us out. If we would be afraid to make our earthly fathers angry, how much more should we fear the God of the Universe?

God created us and sustains us and He deserves to be worshipped and obeyed. We deserve His displeasure, His wrath even, when we don't. But we don't have to continue in His wrath. He loved us enough to provide a way out, if we will only take it.

2

LESSON 2
A PERFECT STANDARD
AND A PERFECT SACRIFICE

Question 85: What does God require of us, that we may escape his wrath and curse, due to us for sin?

Answer: To escape the wrath and curse of God, due to us for sin, God requires of us faith in Jesus Christ, repentance to life, with the diligent use of all the outward means by which Christ communicates to us the benefits of redemption.

Question 86: What is faith in Jesus Christ?

Answer: Faith in Jesus Christ is a saving grace, by which we receive and rest on Him alone for salvation, as He is offered to us in the Gospel.

1. If we receive salvation through Christ, what are we saved from?
   Read 1 Thessalonians 5:9

2. Why do we deserve God's wrath?
   Read Ecclesiastes 7:20; Romans 3:12

3. What does God require as payment for our sins?
   Read Leviticus 5:13-15;5:5-7

4. Why was the death of Christ necessary to satisfy the requirement of a sacrifice for sin?
   Read Hebrews 10:4-10

5. What happens to those who do not accept Christ's death as a sacrifice for their sins?
   Read Revelation 21:8

6. What is the simplest expression of our faith in Christ?
   Read Romans 10:9

7. What else happens when we first believe in Christ?
   Read Mark 1:15

8. What is repentance?
   Read 1 Kings 8:47

9. Are we able to turn to Christ on our own, without help?
   Read John 6:65

10. How are we made able to come to Christ?
    Read 1 Corinthians 12:3

11. How are we to live if we believe in Christ?
    Read James 1:22; Philippians 2:5-8

LESSON 2
A PERFECT STANDARD
AND A PERFECT SACRIFICE

Catechism Questions 85 and 86

YOU MAY BE GETTING TIRED OF READING AND HEARING THAT YOU deserve God's wrath, but there is really no other way to say it—we are all miserable failures at living up to God's demands. We mess up at every turn. Even the good things that we manage to do, we usually do for selfish motives. If we are truly honest with ourselves, we will be very disappointed with the way we live.

God made it crystal clear from the beginning of time that He expected perfection from His creation. From our vantage point, it looks like He made it pretty easy for Adam and Eve—just one rule to obey—but they blew it. I'm not going to go through the whole argument here [I've laid it all out in Book 1, Lesson 6], but suffice it to say, we would have done the same thing. We would all have yielded to the temptation.

So none of us is perfect. Isn't God expecting too much? He has given us a standard that we are incapable of living up to. Isn't that unfair? It depends on how you look at it. I am a teacher. I am actually a pretty demanding teacher. I have fairly strict standards. However, I am also very willing to help any student meet those standards. For example, in my public speaking classes, I require an outline for every speech, and those outlines must adhere to rigid guidelines. However, if a student comes to my office before an outline is due, I will see to it that his or her outline meets every one of the guidelines perfectly. His or her score on the outline will be 100%. If a student writes an outline on his/her own that meets the guidelines, he or she will also score 100%. But if a student decides not to take advantage of my help and the outline does not meet the guidelines, I do not feel guilty for giving that outline the score it deserves. Am I being unfair? Am I overly demanding? Some of those students who get low scores think so. But why were their scores low? First, they did not meet the requirements. But second, they did not ask for help.

Yes, God has impossibly high standards. But He has also promised to give us help in meeting those standards. What did He say about asking for help?

"No temptation has seized you except what is common to man. And God is unpredictable; sometimes, he will not let you be tempted beyond what you can bear. And sometimes, when you are tempted, he will provide a way out." Is that what you believe? Is that what the verse says? Look at 1 Corinthians 10:13. Which words did I change? God is not unpredictable—He is *faithful*. And there is no "sometimes" about it. He will not let you be tempted beyond what you can bear; He will provide a way out. We may say we believe this verse, but we act like we believe my heretical interpretation. Or we believe it, we just don't want a way out. We actually enjoy the temptation and the accompanying sin very much, thank you, and really don't want to think about giving it up. We would much prefer to rationalize that we are only human and are not perfect, anyway.

So we are sinners, and we deserve God's wrath. What is the ultimate result of that wrath for us. It couldn't be that bad, could it? The ultimate result is Hell itself. In graduate school, it was somehow obvious that I was a Christian, or at least that I was really moral. Even though I had not gone out of my way to publicly announce my faith, my fellow grad students were careful not to use profanity around me and to treat me with the utmost respect. Until the subject of Hell came up. One of them finally asked me one day whether I really believed in a literal Heaven, or more importantly, in a literal Hell. I told him that yes, since Jesus taught that there is a Hell, I had no choice but to believe in it. From that moment on, he decided that I was a "religious nut." He still treated me differently, but for different reasons.

What does Jesus say about Hell? He told his disciples that it is an eternal fire, prepared for the devil and his angels, and that there will be darkness and weeping and gnashing of teeth. He also said that those who have not done His will are to be sent there.

This is not a pretty picture, but it is a picture painted by Christ Himself. He wanted us to know that it is a real place, and He wanted us to not want to go there.

So what is God's standard? How do we avoid Hell? By obeying God perfectly. Some of you may be thinking now, "Well, thank you very much.

That is sooo helpful. I am quite sure I can do that. No problem. You might as well have told me to fly to the moon once a month to gather groceries." And I really might as well. We all know we are not going to be able to do that. God would help us do it if we asked, but we know we're not always going to ask. And even if we do ask, we're not always going to follow the instructions we are given.

But fortunately, God knows that too. And for some amazing reason that I absolutely do not understand, God wants us in His Heaven in spite of the way we behave. His love is so great that He provided a way for us to get there when there was no way to do it ourselves. At first, He created a system of sacrificing animals to pay for the sins of the people. These animals had to be perfect specimens of whatever type of animal they were. They had to be sacrificed by a priest, and some of their blood had to be sprinkled on the altar. Once a year, a special day was set aside to pay for the sins of all the people for the whole year—the Day of Atonement. But these sacrifices had to be made over and over. No animal could pay for the sins of a human being forever.

What was required was the sacrifice of a perfect human. It is interesting to me to study different religions. I have found in doing this that every religion has gotten something right; there is an element of truth in every religion. There is much more that is wrong, but there is truth there. Satan has taken the truth and twisted it, but you can find truth in every system of worship. Think about those ancient pagan religions that practiced human sacrifice. How abhorrent! Yet, wasn't this really on the right track? Didn't God require a human sacrifice to pay for our sin? They just weren't relying on the right human.

You see, the only human sacrifice that would do was one that was perfect. Does that mean he or she had to be perfect looking? Not at all. In fact, the Bible tells us that Jesus was not more handsome or majestic than other men [Isaiah 53:2]. God does not judge by outward appearance; He judges the heart. In other words, the perfect human sacrifice had to be perfect in heart, or completely sinless. No such person has ever existed. Every created human being since the first man and woman has sinned. So God Himself came to earth. God the Son took on a human body and was born of a woman. She was a virgin so He would have both a human nature and a divine nature.

With His human nature, He could experience all of the temptations that every other person on earth experiences; but with His divine nature, He could resist them. Since He could resist every temptation, He could be the perfect human sacrifice; and He was willing to do that so that our sins could be paid for.

But God even goes further than that. In order for Christ's death to pay for our sins, we have to accept that payment. Suppose one day, your friend receives an inheritance check for several million dollars. She is an instant multi-millionaire, but only if she will take the check to the bank and deposit the money in her account. Now suppose that when you tell her this, she doesn't believe you. She argues that all she has to do is have the check. For them to require her to bring in the check is too demanding. She does not have time to make a special trip downtown just to confirm what she already knows—she has a multi-million dollar check. So she never takes the check to the bank. As a result, although she can tell everyone she has inherited a great deal of money, she will have nothing to show for it but a bunch of numbers on a piece of paper.

Without God's help, we would treat Christ's death just like this. God tells us that we must accept Christ's death as a sacrifice for our own personal sins; the sacrifice is there, and it is perfectly sufficient to pay for our sins. But we must each accept it personally, or it doesn't count. We can complain that God is being too demanding, or we can ignore Him completely, but our excuses will not matter to God. And the thing is, not one single one of us would accept this sacrifice on our own unless God changed our heart and made us want to do it. That is what Jesus meant when He talked about being "born again." When we are born the first time, we come into this world. When we are born the second time, we come into God's world. We become able to see things from God's perspective. We suddenly want to please God. And the first step in this process is that we want to accept Christ's sacrifice as payment for our sins. So Christ pays for our sins and then sends His Spirit to cause us to want that payment.

We take this for granted, but think for a minute about what this means. The only way for you to escape the fires of Hell was for a perfect human being to be sacrificed to pay for your sins. There are no perfect human beings. So there was no one to sacrifice. But God wanted you in Heaven. In spite of everything you have done to ignore Him, displease Him, frustrate Him, anger Him, etc., He wanted you there. In fact, He wanted you there badly enough to become a man Himself and suffer a cruel, cruel death to make it possible. Then His Spirit works in you to help you to understand just what He has done for you. What kind of love is that?! What kind of response does that kind of love deserve?

3

LESSON 3
REPENTANCE AND GRACE

Question 87: What is repentance to life?

Answer: Repentance to life is a saving grace, by which a sinner, out of a true sense of his sin, and understanding of the mercy of God in Christ, does, with grief and hatred of his sin, turn from it to God, with full intention of, and endeavor after, new obedience.

1. What is the life that true repentance leads us to?
    Read 1 John 5:13; John 10:10

2. The dictionary defines *grace* as "unmerited favor and love" or "favor rendered by one who need not do so."[1] How are these passages examples of these definitions of *grace*?
    Read Ephesians 2:1-10; 2 Timothy 1:9

3. What makes a person a sinner?
    Read Isaiah 42:24; Romans 3:23

4. How do we gain a true sense of our own sin?
    Read Romans 3:20; John 16:7-8

5. How do we gain an understanding of the mercy of God in Christ?
    Read Romans 5:6-8;

6. How are we able to turn from our sins to God?
    Read Romans 8:5-9

7. Can we overcome our sins in our own strength?
    Read Galatians 3:3, 10; Romans 8:3, 5

8. What is the new obedience that we should endeavor after?
    Read 1 John 2:3; Luke 11:28

9. If we are obedient, does this mean that we will never sin?
    Read 1 John 1:8, 10

10. What should we do when we sin?
    Read 1 John 1:9

LESSON 3
REPENTANCE AND GRACE

Catechism Question 87

YOU HAVE ALL PROBABLY SEEN SIGNS ALONG THE ROAD, OR PERHAPS even someone holding a sign, which says, "Repent!" The problem is that those signs rarely tell us what we are to repent from or how exactly we are to accomplish that repentance. But since Jesus Himself told us to repent, this is not a concept that we can dismiss out of hand.

What exactly is repentance, and how can we achieve it?

While still a very young man, Benjamin Franklin, determined, as he put it, to "arrive at moral perfection." He "wished to live without committing any fault at any time."

He identified twelve Virtues by which a moral man should live; and when a Quaker friend commented on his pride, he added a thirteenth Virtue of humility. This is Franklin's list:

1. TEMPERANCE: Eat not to dullness. Drink not to elevation.
2. SILENCE: Speak not but what may benefit others or yourself. Avoid trifling conversation.
3. ORDER: Let all your things have their places. Let each part of your business have its time.
4. RESOLUTION: Resolve to perform what you ought. Perform without fail what you resolve.
5. FRUGALITY: Make no expense but to do good to others or yourself, i.e., waste nothing.
6. INDUSTRY: Lose no time. Be always employed in something useful. Cut off all unnecessary actions.
7. SINCERITY: Use no hurtful deceit. Think innocently and justly; if you speak, speak accordingly.
8. JUSTICE: Wrong none by doing injuries or omitting the benefits that are your duty.

9. MODERATION: Avoid extremes. Forbear resenting injuries so much as you think they deserve.

10. CLEANLINESS: Tolerate no uncleanliness in body, clothes, or habitation.

11. TRANQUILITY: Be not disturbed at trifles or at accidents common or unavoidable.

12. CHASTITY: Rarely use venery [sexual pleasure] but for health or offspring—never to dullness, weakness, or the injury of your own or another's peace or reputation.

13. HUMILITY: Imitate Jesus and Socrates.[2]

Franklin chose the order of the Virtues very carefully. He placed Temperance first, reasoning that once he had conquered that virtue, the others would be easier to attain. Each of the succeeding virtues were meant to make the ones after it easier to accomplish. Franklin focused on one virtue per week, and kept a notebook in which he noted his progress and marked his failures for the day.

What Franklin discovered was that he "was surpris'd to find myself so much fuller of Faults than I had imagined." To avoid having to use new notebooks, or scraping off the ink in the old notebook, which would soon leave it full of holes, "I mark'd my Faults with a black Lead Pencil, which Marks I could easily wipe out with a wet Sponge."[3]

You are probably not surprised at Franklin's failure to achieve his goal. No mere human being can achieve moral perfection on his own. In fact, on a website encouraging young people to follow Franklin's example, the author writes, "The thirteen virtues are a good guide for you to follow. In fact, keeping track of how well you do in maintaining the virtues and having positive character traits, as Franklin did, is worth trying. You also need to realize that no one is perfect. The main idea is to follow the advice of Benjamin Franklin and try to be a person of good character."[4]

What Franklin was attempting was a type of repentance, but it was not repentance to life. So where did our beloved founding father go wrong?

First, he was using the wrong list. God had already given us a list of rules that we are to follow perfectly. That list is hard enough; we certainly don't need another one. By creating his own list, Franklin was acting as his own god, and establishing his own "Thirteen Commandments." Some of Franklin's "Commandments" do relate to God's law, but notice how vastly they differ. And ironically, even though Franklin made up his own laws, even he was not able to obey them.

Second, Franklin refused to call a sin a sin. He merely saw his failures as moral shortcomings which could be overcome by his own personal diligence. Franklin had a sense of sin, but he did not acknowledge it as sin. He developed his list of virtues out of his own sense of morality, which in some cases went in direct contradiction to the law of God. Look at Virtue number 12. Do you see the idea of marriage anywhere in that statement? If you read about Franklin's personal life, you will understand why. His first son was born out of wedlock, and there is serious question whether he and his wife were ever really legally married. In my opinion, Franklin did the honorable thing by raising his oldest son in his home and treating him as legitimate, but the point is that he apparently saw nothing wrong with the circumstances surrounding that son's birth.

Third, Franklin tried to accomplish moral perfection on his own power. Although he believed in God, he did not turn to God to help him in his quest. Franklin wrote a letter shortly before his death in which he stated that his view of Jesus Christ was that he believed in His system of morals and His religion, but he also "understood" that it had been corrupted. Franklin said that he had doubts about the divinity of Christ but that he had not studied it and would not do so "when I expect soon an opportunity of knowing the truth with less trouble." He also did not believe that God looked upon unbelievers in the world with any particular displeasure.[5]

A man with such a belief about God and Christ would not be quick to ask for their assistance in becoming a better person. And in light of his thoughts about unbelievers, he would not be likely to think that God would care. How sad for Dr. Franklin! But fortunately, we are not condemned to live as he did. We can have the same goal—to live a morally pure life--but we can have the aid of an all-powerful God as we go through the process of trying to attain it.

Of course, we won't attain it any more than Dr. Franklin did. And that is his fourth mistake. He actually thought he could do it! He did not understand the total sinfulness of man. He really thought that by focusing on one virtue per week, after a few years of practice, he could become perfect. And he was surprised at how often he failed. Our advantage, if you will, is that we know we can't do it. We know that we are supposed to try, but we are not surprised when we don't make it. We are not discouraged or disillusioned because we know that we are sinful people and that we will never attain perfection in this life.

So what's the point of repentance? Well, there are two ways in which you can repent. The first way is one that I don't think Dr. Franklin ever tried, unless it was at the very end of his life; if he had, his whole list of virtues might never have been made. That is the turning away from our sin nature, *in general*, and turning to God. That happens the moment we come to Christ, when we are born again. Scripture teaches us that the only way we are able to do this is because the Holy Spirit changes our nature, making us able to repent and believe in Christ. So the only way we can repent in the first place is because of God and Him alone.

This should not be taken lightly. None of us wants God. We love our sins, and we do not want to give them up. We are unable, on our own, to choose God. That is why Jesus told us, "No one can come to me unless the Father who sent me draws him" [John 6:44]. And "No one can come to me unless the Father has enabled him." [John 6:65] Without the Holy Spirit's first changing our hearts, we would forever reject Christ. But if we believe, then the Holy Spirit has changed us and enabled us to repent and believe. We have turned from love of sin to love of Christ.

Now that is true in a general sense, in the sense that leads to salvation. But does that mean that we no longer sin? Of course not. If we were to keep a notebook like Dr. Franklin's and make a mark every time we fail, we would find, just as he did, that it is soon full of marks. Our sin nature still needs to be conquered. In one sense it has been conquered. But in another sense, it is still there tempting us to go astray.

So that is the other meaning for the idea of repentance—daily, or by the minute, turning from our sins and turning to God. Whenever we are tempted, we are to turn to God, who has promised that He will always provide a way of escape. And if we do sin, we are to confess our sins with the assurance that we will be forgiven. But we don't have to do this alone either. The Holy Spirit is still there, guiding us along the right path, warning us when there is trouble ahead, and admonishing us when we have gotten off the path entirely. Unlike Benjamin Franklin, we have lots of help, and it is help of the most powerful kind. The God who created the universe walks with us each step of the way and will be there every minute to offer help and encouragement. All we have to do is listen and follow.

4

LESSON 4
THE WORD OF GOD

Question 88: What are the outward means by which Christ communicates to us the benefits of redemption?

Answer: The outward and ordinary means by which Christ communicates to us the benefits of redemption are His ordinances, especially the Word, sacraments, and prayer, all of which are made effectual to the elect for salvation.

1. What is meant by the Word?
    Read 2 Peter 1:20-21

2. What are the sacraments?
    Read Matthew 28:19; 1 Corinthians 11:23-26

3. What is the best example of how to pray?
    Read Matthew 6:9-13

4. Who are the elect?
   Read Mark 13:20; 1 Peter 2:9; 2 Timothy 2:10

Question 89: How is the Word made effectual to salvation?

Answer: The Spirit of God makes the reading, but especially the preaching, of the Word an effectual means of convincing and converting sinners, and of building them up in holiness and comfort, through faith to salvation.

5. Who is described as preaching in the New Testament?
   Read Matthew 4:23; Mark 1:4; Luke 9:1-2; Acts 8:25, 40; Acts 17:13

6. What did Paul tell Timothy to do in his absence?
   Read 1 Timothy 4:13

7. Why is preaching necessary?
   Read Romans 10:14

Question 90: How is the Word to be read and heard, that it may become effectual to salvation?

Answer: That the Word may become effectual to salvation we must attend to it with diligence, preparation, and prayer; receive it with faith and love; lay it up in our hearts; and practice it in our lives.

8. How do we attend to the Word with diligence?
   Read 2 Peter 1:19; Proverbs 8:34

9. How should we prepare and pray to hear or read the Word?
   Read Psalm 119:18

10. How are we to receive the Word?
    Read Luke 8:15; Psalm 119:42

11. Why is it important to lay up the Word in our hearts?
    Read Psalm 119:11; Hebrews 12:5

12. Is listening to or reading the Word enough?
    Read James 1:22

LESSON 4
THE WORD OF GOD

Catechism Questions 88, 89, and 90

I WAS RECENTLY DIAGNOSED WITH A MEDICAL CONDITION. IT ISN'T LIFE-threatening, but it does require some attention on my part or it will affect my lifestyle. My doctor gave me a booklet to read that tells me what to do to deal with this condition most effectively. Two things concern me: I have to take daily medication and I am supposed to exercise. I am not fond of living on medication and I really do not like to exercise, so how do I know I can trust this booklet? What if the people who wrote it had some ulterior motives? What if they own stock in a pharmaceutical company or a fitness center? I think I'll just ignore the whole thing. Besides, I think I heard somewhere that medical booklets are unreliable anyway.

So what do you think of my decision? If you are a rational, sensible person, you probably think I'm nuts. Exercise is good for me, and taking one little pill is not going to ruin my day. Why would I doubt the accuracy of the booklet? The only reason I can think of is that I don't like some of what's in there. I am trying to rationalize the fact that I am not following the instructions by discrediting the source.

That's what lots of folks do with the Bible. They don't like some of what's in there, so they try to discredit the source. In this lesson, I first want to explore several arguments for the accuracy of the Bible. Then I want to talk about our response to the Bible.

First, let's look at how we can know that the Bible is really the Word of God. I cannot possibly go into these arguments in detail, so I will give you some websites that you can consult on your own if you would like more information. We will look at four arguments: the argument from prophecy, the argument from history, the argument from science, and the argument from eyewitnesses.

The Bible is full of prophecies, predictions of events that would happen in the future. In contrast to every other prophet or prophetic book, every event that the Bible has predicted to happen by now has actually happened. Let me repeat that. Every single one of the prophecies that should have happened has happened. There was not one mistake. This is not true of any other supposed prophet. I see many magazine articles about the prophecies of Nostradamus, but not only are his prophecies vague, they are often completely wrong. For instance, according to many people, he predicted that the world would end in 1999. The prophecies of the Bible have never been wrong. Not once.

The book of Micah was written approximately 700 years before the birth of Jesus, yet he prophesied that the Messiah, the Savior, would be born in Bethlehem. This was remarkable because Bethlehem was not much of a town. It was a historic city, the home of David, but it was not the seat of government or a prominent place in Israel. In fact, Micah calls it "the least" or "little." It would not have been the most likely place for such an important person to be born. But it was true. Jesus, who is called the Messiah, was born in Bethlehem.

Likewise, the book of Isaiah was written almost 700 years before Christ's birth, but he prophesied exactly what would happen to Jesus. He describes Him as a man of sorrows who is led to His death without uttering a word in His defense. He even explains that He took on our sins and paid for our iniquities. All of this was fulfilled in Jesus' trials before Herod and Pontius Pilate and His agonizing death on the cross. Isaiah did not know that His name would be Jesus, but he accurately portrayed what He would do for His people.

These are only two of hundreds of prophecies in the Bible that have already been fulfilled. So one reason we can trust the Bible is its record of 100% accuracy in predicting the future. Mere man has never achieved that result; someone or something else must have been involved. Of course that someone else is God.

A second argument for the truth of the Bible is the argument from history. For many years, historians and archeologists argued that the Bible included people and places that were not mentioned anywhere else, and that it therefore could not be trusted. However, the more we have discovered through archeology, the more the accuracy of the Bible has been proved. For example, the tribe of the Hittites was believed to be a non-existent group until the early twentieth century, when an archeological excavation discovered remains of the culture in Bogazkoy, Turkey. Similarly, the Assyrian king Sargon was thought to be mythological until French archeologists found his royal city in Khorsabad, Iraq, in the nineteenth century. Dr. Nelson Glueck, Biblical Archaeologist and President of the Hebrew Union College-Jewish Institute of Religion, is quoted as saying, "No archeological discovery has ever controverted a Biblical reference. Scores of archeological findings have been made which confirm in clear outline or in exact detail historical statements in the Bible."[6]

So according to archeology and history, the Bible is overwhelmingly accurate. Even people and places that were thought to be non-existent have recently been found. If the Bible mentions people and places that men did not even know about, who do you think did know? Which leads us to argument three: the argument from science. Not only did God know about people and places, He also had scientific knowledge that man did not have at the time the Bible was written.

In about 1600 B.C., Job told us that the earth hangs on nothing. This is common knowledge today, but in ancient Mesopotamia, where Job lived, the world was believed to be a flat disk floating in the ocean. At the same time, the Hindus believed that the earth was supported by four elephants, the ancient Greeks believed that the god Atlas carried the earth on his shoulders, and the Egyptians thought the earth rested on crystal spheres. The first people to advance the theory that the earth was a sphere were Pythagorus and Thales of Miletus in the 500's B.C. Likewise, the first theory that the earth floated in space was not until the 500's B.C., and we didn't really understand how gravity held the earth in place until Sir Isaac Newton published his theories in 1687 A.D. This means that hundreds or even thousands of years passed before scientific knowledge caught up with what Job said in the Bible.

The next two verses in Job deal with wind and water. Job also refers to the weight of the wind. According to NASA, the fact that air has weight was not discovered until the year 1640 A.D. That is over 2,000 years after Job made his statement. How did he know this? It was also in the 1600's that people understood that rain is produced from water that has evaporated from lakes, rivers, and even the oceans. But the book of Job explained this thousands of years earlier. I think it is safe to assume that either the writers of the Bible were incredibly advanced scientifically or that God Himself had a hand in writing the Bible.

Finally, let's look at the Bible from the argument of eyewitness accounts. John says in his gospel account, "We have seen His glory." Paul tells us in his first letter to the Corinthians that after His resurrection, Jesus appeared to more than five hundred people, most of whom were still alive when he wrote the letter. These men appealed to the fact that there were eyewitnesses of what they were writing about who were still alive and who could testify for or against the accuracy of the reports. There is no record that any eyewitness accused either man of speaking falsely or even stretching the truth.

So I have given you four arguments. In light of fulfilled prophecies, historical accuracy, scientific knowledge that pre-dates that of "science" itself, and eyewitness accounts, what conclusion should we come to? The only logical conclusion is that there is more to this book than just a book. It is undoubtedly the work of God Himself.

So what are we to do with this knowledge? If the Bible is the actual Word of God, how should it affect our lives? First of all, it should be taken seriously. When we read or hear the Word of God, we should focus on the Word and the Word alone. We should find a place free of other distractions and concentrate on what we are hearing or reading.

I am a real fan of mystery novels, but I try to stay away from the really creepy ones. Once, by accident, I started one that scared the pants off of me —not because it was particularly violent, but because of the location and circumstances of the crime. A woman was led into a vast underground cavern, and then left there alone to die. I have been on tours of underground caves where the guide turned out all of the lights to show us how dark total darkness truly is. The idea of being left alone in such a situation is completely horrifying to me. Fortunately, in the novel, the woman was rescued. When she saw her rescuers coming, she almost attacked them in her eagerness to get to the light.

This should really be our attitude toward the Word of God. We live in a world of total darkness. Most of those around us have no concept of who God really is and no guidance from His Holy Spirit. As we try to move and live in that world, we should run almost screaming and crying in our eagerness to get the truth and the light that is given to us in Scripture. It is our only lifeline to what is real and true and what will save us from the horrors of the world in which we now live.

Then second, we should believe it and act on it. It is not enough to just read or hear the Word; we must also obey it. We should try to memorize key Scripture passages so that we can recall them at times when our Bible isn't handy and we need to be reminded of what God has told us. If memorizing Scripture is hard for you, then don't try to learn long passages. Focus on short bits that have great meaning for you. "When you walk through the fire, I will be with you," for example. Or "I know the plans I have for you; plans for good and not for evil." Those are not difficult passages, but they can bring great comfort to an anxious soul.

Third, and maybe most important, the Word needs to be preached. This is the means that God has chosen for conveying His Word to those who do not yet know Him. He could have called people to Himself in a number of ways, and He has used other ways on occasion. But the primary means that God uses for spreading His Word is the preaching and teaching of it. And He has promised that His Word will not return to Him without accomplishing its purpose. If we are given the opportunity to teach the Word of God, we should do so humbly, in total dependence on God, and be very careful that what we say and do are in complete agreement with what He says in His Word.

God's Word is exactly what the phrase implies—the actual words of God Himself. He has chosen to speak to us directly through the pages of Scripture and through the mouths of those He has chosen to preach and teach His Word. Let's be careful to focus on what He has to say and to apply it to our lives on a daily basis.

If you would like more information on the arguments for the accuracy of the Bible, I found the following websites to be very useful. I hope they are still active:

http://www.clarifyingchristianity.com/science.shtml

http://www.christiananswers.net/q-eden/edn-t003.html

http://www.faithfacts.org/search-for-truth/questions-of-christians/how-do-you-know-that-the-bible-is-true

5

LESSON 5

THE SACRAMENT OF BAPTISM

Question 91: How do the sacraments become effectual means of salvation?

Answer: The sacraments become effectual means of salvation, not from any virtue in them, or in him who administers them, but only by the blessing of Christ, and the working of His Spirit in those who by faith receive them.

1. How does the Holy Spirit work in those who receive Christ?
   Read Luke 12:11-12; John 14:26; Acts 1:8; Romans 5:5

Question 92: What is a sacrament?

Answer: A sacrament is a holy ordinance instituted by Christ, in which, by perceptible signs, Christ and the benefits of the new covenant are represented, sealed, and applied to believers.

Question 93: What are the sacraments of the New Testament?

Answer: The sacraments of the New Testament are Baptism and the Lord's Supper.

2. How did Christ institute the sacrament of Baptism?
   Read Matthew 28:19

3. How did Christ institute the sacrament of the Lord's Supper?
   Read Matthew 26:19-20; 26-28

Question 94: What is Baptism?

Answer: Baptism is a sacrament, in which the washing with water, in the name of the Father, and of the Son, and of the Holy Spirit, does signify and seal our grafting into Christ and receiving of the benefits of the Covenant of Grace, and our engagement to be the Lord's.

4. Who told us to baptize in the name of the Father and of the Son and of the Holy Spirit?
   Read Matthew 28:18-19

5. Is it possible to be saved if you are not baptized?
   Read Luke 23:39-43

Question 95: To whom is Baptism to be administered?

Answer: Baptism is not to be administered to any who are out of the visible church, till they profess their faith in Christ and obedience to Him; but the infants of those who are members of the visible Church are to be baptized.

6. What is required for an adult to be baptized?
   Read Acts 8:12, 13

7. What was the sign of the covenant between God and man in the Old Testament?
   Read Genesis 17:9-11

8. Who participated in the covenant sign of circumcision?
   Read Genesis 17: 12

9. Is the covenant between God and man still represented by the sign of circumcision?
   Read Galatians 5:2-6

10. What is now the sign of our covenant with God?
    Read Acts 2:41

11. Were children baptized in the New Testament?
    Read Acts 16:15, 33

12. When the Ethiopian eunuch was baptized, who "went down
    into the water"?
    Read Acts 8:36-38

13. What happened when the apostles received the baptism of the
    Holy Spirit?
    Read Acts 1:5; 2:1-4

14. Have you been baptized? If not, why not? If so, what does your
    baptism mean to you?

LESSON 5
THE SACRAMENT OF BAPTISM

Catechism Questions 91, 92, 93, 94, and 95

DO YOU REMEMBER YOUR OWN BAPTISM? IF YOU WERE BAPTIZED AS AN older child or as an adult, undoubtedly you do. But if you're like me, there is no way you would remember it. I was baptized when I was only a few months old. There are many questions that go along with the subject of baptism, and the purpose of this lesson is to answer those questions the best I can according to the theological perspective of the *Westminster Confession of Faith*. If you have been taught another view of baptism, I ask that you be open-minded as you consider my arguments and that you try to separate tradition from Scriptural instruction.

First of all, in whose name(s) are we to be baptized? For many of us, this is pretty clear, but there is a school of thought that says that since Peter said that we should be baptized in Jesus' name [Acts 2:38], our baptism should be in Jesus' name only. I have two problems with this. First, I don't think Peter was trying to supplant Christ's instructions about baptism. Notice in Matthew 28:19, Jesus says that we are to baptize in the name [singular] of the Father, Son, and Holy Spirit. There is one name, but three persons. I think that Peter was trying to emphasize that baptism should coincide with our belief in Christ. John the Baptist had been baptizing for forgiveness of sins, and others also had been baptizing. Peter wanted us to identify baptism with becoming part of Christ's kingdom. But even if Peter had been arguing that we should be baptized in Jesus' name only, whom should we follow? Christ or Peter? I'm not even going to answer that question.

Second, is baptism necessary for salvation? There are denominations that say that it is. But through the example of the dying thief on the cross, I think Christ has taught us that baptism is not essential. There was absolutely no way that the thief could have been baptized, and yet Christ told him that he would enter paradise. If a person has no opportunity to be baptized, the lack of baptism will not hinder her salvation. However, if a person has the opportunity to be baptized and chooses not to do so, such a choice would leave serious doubt as to her decision to follow and obey Christ. He made it clear that we are to be baptized when we believe.

Third, should everyone be baptized? Any adult or older child who has not made a sincere profession of faith should not be baptized. Furthermore, there is no age at which a child should suddenly make a profession of faith and be baptized. My three daughters came to know the Lord at the ages of 3, 2 ½ , and 6 years of age. [In case you are wondering about those very young ages, I had a long talk with my pastor at the time about the validity of those professions. He agreed with me that they were genuine.] Many churches have a confirmation class and ceremony, which sometimes includes believers' baptism, at around 8 years of age. I think they would have a hard time defending that practice from Scripture. Nowhere in the Bible can you find that 8 years of age, or any other age, is the age at which children come to know the Lord.

So what about children? Can we baptize them, and when should we baptize them? This is perhaps the most divisive issue in the Christian church regarding baptism, so let's look at the argument in favor of infant baptism. In the Old Testament, God gave Abraham the sign of circumcision to designate that a man was a part of the nation of Israel, the chosen nation of God. These people were to believe, love, and obey God. Male children as young as eight days old were to be given this sign. Did that mean that those infants could understand the commandments of God and agree to obey them? Of course not. It meant that those children were included in the covenant God had made with Abraham, that He would be their God and they would be His people. As they grew older, it would be up to each of them to believe and obey God. The sign of circumcision did not save them, but it did set them apart as God's people.

In the New Testament, the sign of circumcision was abolished. In its place, the sign that a person has believed in Jesus and is willing to obey Him is baptism. We now have a new sign for a new covenant, but this sign still signifies that God will be our God and we will be His people. So should it be a sign given to infants? Since the first Christian converts were Jews, who were accustomed to the sign of circumcision being given to infants, don't you think God would have told them explicitly if the new sign of baptism were not to be applied in the same manner? God very explicitly told them that circumcision was no longer necessary. Would He not also have told them that no longer were infants to be included in the sign of the covenant?

But why would God have stopped including infants in His covenant family? They were included in the Old Testament covenant—why not in the New Covenant as well? Infants who are born into Christian families are still a part of the family of God. The sign has changed, but I doubt seriously that God's relationship with the youngest of His children has changed as well.

Finally, we have examples in Scripture where entire households and families were baptized. Surely there were some young children or infants in those families. Since the practice in the Old Testament was to apply the sign of the covenant to very young children, and since God has never told us not to baptize our children, then I think it is very safe to assume that He means for us to continue to do so.

This leads to the fourth question: How are people to be baptized? There are many Christians who believe that baptism must be done by immersion. This leads them to think that obviously this would preclude baptizing young children, since they cannot be immersed. [Actually, some churches do immerse babies, so that argument doesn't hold up even on a practical level.] But does baptism mean that one must be immersed? The Greek word baptism can mean "to immerse," but it can also mean "to pour" or "to sprinkle." In many instances, the word for "sprinkle" or "anoint" in the Old Testament is the same as the word for baptism. Also, as you have seen in Acts Chapter 2, the apostles were baptized by the Holy Spirit through tongues of fire. They were not immersed in fire; fire appeared above their heads and settled on them. The word baptism in this instance clearly does not mean "to immerse." Also, when Phillip baptized the Ethiopian, Scripture tells us that they both "went down into the water." If this phrase means that the Ethiopian was immersed, then Phillip was immersed as well. If this is our understanding of this passage, then every pastor who baptizes by immersion should go under the water with every person he baptizes.

The writers of the *Westminster Confession of Faith* understood the importance of baptism, and they also understood how it should be applied. All adult believers should be baptized to show that they have believed in Christ and that they are now part of the Covenant with God. When we baptize our children, we are showing that they are also a part of the family of God; but just as circumcised children in the Old Testament, they must grow up and establish their own personal relationship with God. Baptism of a child does not save that child; every person must acknowledge for himself that Jesus is Lord and agree to follow and obey Him. The manner of baptism is not significant; we can be immersed or we can be sprinkled. The sign of baptism is what is important because it sets us apart from the world as children of God.

6

LESSON 6

THE SACRAMENT OF THE LORD'S SUPPER

Question 96: What is the Lord's Supper?

Answer: The Lord's Supper is a sacrament, in which by giving and receiving bread and wine, according to Christ's direction, His death is shown forth; and the worthy receivers are, not after a corporal and carnal manner, but by faith, made partakers of His body and blood, with all His benefits, to their spiritual nourishment and growth in grace.

1. When was the Lord's Supper instituted?
    Read Matthew 26:18-30

2. What does the bread of the Lord's Supper represent?
    Read Matthew 26:26

3. What does the wine of the Lord's Supper represent?
    Read Matthew 26:27-28

Question 97: What is required to be worthy of receiving the Lord's Supper?

Answer: It is required of those who would receive the Lord's Supper worthily that they examine themselves, as to their knowledge to discern the Lord's body, as to their faith to feed on Him, and as to their repentance, love, and new obedience; lest, coming unworthily, they eat and drink judgment on themselves.

4. How were the Corinthians observing the Lord's Supper?
    Read 1 Corinthians 11:21

5. What did this show about their attitudes toward God and others?
    Read 1 Corinthians 11:22

6. What are we to do before eating the bread and drinking the wine?
    Read 1 Corinthians 11:28

7. How does Paul tell the Corinthians to behave when observing the Lord's Supper?
    Read 1 Corinthians 11:33-34

8. What happens when we eat the bread and drink the wine?
    Read 1 Corinthians 11:26

9. Did Jesus tell us how often we are to observe the Lord's Supper?
    Read 1 Corinthians 11:25-26

10. Where did Paul receive the instructions he gives us concerning the Lord's Supper?
    Read 1 Corinthians 11:23

11. With what attitude do you come to the Lord's Supper?

42

LESSON 6
THE SACRAMENT OF THE LORD'S SUPPER

Catechism Questions 96 and 97

"THE LORD'S SUPPER." WHAT DO THOSE WORDS BRING TO MIND? IN many churches, this sacrament is celebrated with tiny pieces of bread or wafers and tiny little cups full of grape juice or wine. In others, a full loaf of bread is used with a large cup of wine or juice which is shared by everyone. In this lesson we will explore the meaning of this sacrament and the proper attitude toward its celebration.

When Christ instituted what we call the "Lord's Supper," it may have been during a Passover meal. This is a full meal, not the traditional bit of bread and taste of wine or juice that we commonly use in our communion services today. This will be important to remember later. Each element in the meal has special significance. The order of the meal would be as follows:

1. Light the Passover candles and recite two blessings over the candles as you light them.

2. Bless the wine, and then pour a cup for each guest and a cup for the prophet Elijah. Everyone drinks the first cup, which symbolizes God's promise to take His people out of Egypt. Then pour the second cup. Elijah's cup will remain untouched.

3. Wash your hands, then eat parsley or some other green vegetable dipped in salt water. The vegetable symbolizes rebirth and the salt water is symbolic of the tears shed by the Jews held in slavery in Egypt.

4. There will be a pile of three matzohs (pieces of unleavened bread) on the table. Break the middle one and return half of it to the pile. Hide the other half. Later, the children will hunt for it and eat it.

5. Tell the story of the exodus from Egypt and the first Passover. At the end of the story, recite a blessing over the second cup of wine and drink it. This cup represents God's promise to deliver the Hebrews from slavery.

6. Wash your hands and say a blessing, then recite two blessings over the matzoh. Eat a piece of matzoh after saying the blessings.

7. Recite a blessing over a bitter vegetable (usually raw horseradish), symbolizing the bitterness of slavery. Dip the bitter vegetable into a paste called charoset (made of chopped nuts, cinnamon, and apples) and eat it. Then make a sandwich using another piece of bitter vegetable and charoset between two small pieces of matzoh.

8. Eat a festive meal. During this time, the children hunt for the hidden piece of matzoh.

9. Pour the third cup of wine, recite a grace after the meal, then bless and drink the wine. This is the cup of redemption, and it represents God's promise to redeem His people. Then pour a fourth cup of wine for everyone. Have a child open a door for the prophet Elijah, who is supposed to arrive on Passover to announce the coming of the Messiah.

10. Recite a series of psalms and a blessing over the last cup of wine, representing God's promise to acquire Israel as a nation, and drink the fourth cup of wine.

11. Announce that the Passover celebration has been completed and that you wish to celebrate it next year in Jerusalem, which is a wish that for the Messiah to come.

Again, notice that this is a meal. Whether it was a Passover meal or not, Jesus and His disciples ate a full meal in the upper room on the last night before His crucifixion. Since it was Passover week, when He referred to the bread, He was probably referring to matzoh, or unleavened bread. When He spoke of the wine, most scholars agree that He was talking about the third cup of wine in the Seder meal, the symbol of God's promise to redeem His people. He was saying that from that time forward, whenever anyone partook of this meal, they should remember that the promise to redeem was fulfilled in Him. They should also remember that the middle piece of matzoh, the piece that was broken and hidden (ie, buried) was also a representation of Himself.

When Paul wrote his instructions about the observation of the Lord's Supper, this was apparently still the practice; the Christians were still eating the full meal of the Passover. However, they were doing so to satisfy their own appetites and not to glorify God. Apparently, when they gathered to observe this meal, these Christians were not following the patterns set out for them, but they were each eating and drinking as they pleased. Some were taking more than they should and leaving nothing for others.

After admonishing them for their behavior, Paul reminds them of what had happened when Jesus instituted the Lord's Supper and that this observance is meant as a proclamation of the death of the Lord Jesus Christ. He then cautions them again not to eat the bread or drink the wine in an unworthy manner, but to examine themselves to be certain that their motives are pure in taking part.

It is important for us to understand the historical significance of the Passover, the basis of the Lord's Supper, to fully understand the admonition Paul is giving us. What are we to examine ourselves about?

First, we are to be sure that we have received a new birth through the Holy Spirit and that we understand what we are doing. We must understand that Christ died as a substitute for our sins and that only through Him can we receive eternal life.

Second, we must be sure that we have repented of a life of sin and are endeavoring to the best of our abilities to live as Christ would have us live. We must desire to follow Christ. We must trust in Him to guide and direct our lives.

Third, we must be sure that we have no unconfessed sin. Maybe. It depends on what you mean by "unconfessed sin." If you mean that a person must have confessed and repented of every sin he has committed, then no, that is not a requirement for participating in the Lord's Supper. There is no one alive who is even aware of all of his sins, let alone has confessed all of them. "Eating the bread or drinking the cup in an unworthy manner" does not mean that we are sinless, or even aware of all of our sins. However, if you mean that a person has a sin or sins that he is very much aware of, but is not ready to repent of, to give up, then I would say that he should not participate. Such a person is not really trying to follow Christ to the best of his abilities. But remember that this admonition was given by Paul primarily so that we would not behave as he has described in verse 21 of 1 Corinthians 11.

So what happens when we receive the Lord's Supper in an appropriate manner? First of all, Scripture tells us that by doing so, we are proclaiming to everyone around us the death of Jesus Christ for our sins. This observance is a visible reminder of what Christ did on the cross. As His body was beaten and broken and His blood was shed for our sins, the bread and wine are visible representations of His love for us.

Second, we are connected spiritually in a special way with Christ. We do not believe that the bread and wine actually become the physical body and blood of Christ; but we do believe that He is spiritually present in these elements, and that when we eat and drink them, we have a special communion (intimate communication) with Christ.

So how often should we do this? There is a great deal of debate over this question, and different churches have answered it in different ways. Some churches observe the Lord's Supper every Sunday; others once a month; others a few times a year. Since Scripture does not specify how often a group is to observe this Supper, I would not presume to dictate a specific time frame. The important thing is that it should be done, and it should be done with reverence and with full attention to the significance of the event.

Scripture does not tell us to examine our denomination, our church, or even our family. We are told to examine ourselves. Next time you have a chance to participate in the Lord's Supper, examine your motives for doing so. If your desire is to live in a way that is pleasing to Christ, and if you are participating to strengthen your relationship with Him, that is all He asks.

7

LESSON 7
PRAYER

Question 98: What is prayer?

Answer: Prayer is an offering up of our desires to God, for things agreeable to His will, in the name of Christ, with confession of our sins, and thankful acknowledgment of His mercies.

1. What does prayer involve?
    Read 2 Chronicles 6:21; 30:27; Nehemiah 1:6; 11:17

2. What kinds of things can we ask God for in prayer?
    Read Psalm 5:2; 6:9; Jeremiah 42:3; 2 Chronicles 6:29; James 5:16; Matthew 26:41; 1 Timothy 5:5

3. What kinds of things did Paul pray for?
    Read Romans 1:10; 15:31; 2 Corinthians 13:9; Ephesians 3:16-18; 6:19

4. What promises do we have that God will hear our prayers?
   Read Deuteronomy 4:7; 2 Chronicles 7:14

5. What if our prayers are not answered immediately?
   Read Luke 18:1

6. How should we pray?
   Read Matthew 6:6-7

7. What if we don't know what to pray for?
   Read Romans 8:26

8. What result can we expect from prayer?
   Read Philippians 4:6-7

9. How can we know our prayers will work?
   Read James 5:16

LESSON 7
PRAYER

Catechism Question 98

HAVE YOU EVER HEARD A YOUNG CHILD PRAY? "GOD BLESS MOMMY and daddy and grandmommy and granddaddy and all my friends and keep me safe all through the night. Amen." Isn't that beautiful?

How about an adult? "God bless all my family and friends and help me to earn more money and get that promotion I have been wanting. Heal all my aches and pains and please keep my car from breaking down. Please don't let the bad economy ruin my 401K, and provide a way for me to go on vacation this year. In Jesus' name, Amen."

What happened? When do we become so selfish? Is that how you pray? (Be honest.)

In this lesson, we will look at prayer in general, then in the next few lessons we will look more specifically at the Lord's Prayer. So first of all, what is prayer? Richard Pratt, in his book *Pray With Your Eyes Open*,[7] defines prayer as "a believer's communication with God." Since I teach communication, I particularly like this definition. In communication studies, it is generally understood that in order for communication to take place, there must be three elements present: a source of the communication, a receiver of the communication, and a message that is being communicated. There are more elements, but these are the essential three. So let's look at each of the elements as they apply to a believer's prayer.

First is the source of the communication—the person who is praying. I would venture to say that most of us could do with a more vibrant and active prayer life, so let's first look at reasons we may have for failing to pray as we should. In the book *Plain Talk on Prayer*, Manford Gutzke[8] gives us five reasons:

- Ignorance—We don't realize we can or need to pray. We become so accustomed to trying to do things on our own that we don't even think about praying.

- Indifference—We don't expect God to act. We forget that He is the God of the Universe who loves us. He can do whatever He desires, and He desires the best for us.

- Indolence—We are too lazy to pray. We will not make the time or use the mental energy to pray as we ought.

- Irresponsibility—We decide that "it's not my problem." We live in our own little world; if it doesn't affect us directly, we aren't concerned

- Indwelling sin—We don't want to come face to face with God. We are unwilling to confront our sin and ask for God's forgiveness; we are unwilling to repent.

Do any of these apply to you? That could be your first matter of prayer—talk to God about letting go of that particular sinful attitude.

We must also think about how often we pray. Scripture tells us to pray without ceasing. What does that mean for us? In my opinion, it means that God and His concerns must be first in our minds and hearts; we must continually see the world and those in it through His eyes. We can keep up a running conversation with God about the things we see, hear, and experience to know how to deal with those things. However, it can also help to set aside specific times during the day to pray.

So we ourselves are the source of the communication of prayer, and a lot of us are not doing a very good job of it. But when we do pray, who is the receiver of the communication? The Lord Almighty, the Creator of the Universe, who is also the Father of all who believe. If you are a believer in Christ, then think about what God has done for you. Through His death and resurrection, Jesus has opened the way for us to have direct access to God. He is also our High Priest and represents us before the heavenly altar, praying for us. Search the Scripture to learn all you can about who God is. Pratt cautions us that if we have a limited concept of God, our prayers can become repetitious and boring. The better you know God, the more you will pray to Him and the more intimate your prayers will be.

The third element of communication is the message itself—the prayer. In order to understand what prayer is, I think it might be helpful if we first understand what it is not. In this, I can definitely not set myself up as an example. I have prayed for a better understanding of prayer so that I could write this study, and I think God has answered that prayer. In fact, I am now convinced that my prayer life falls so short of what it should be that I hesitate to even write this at all. So this is without a doubt a "do what I say, not what I do" type of lesson.

First of all, prayer is not a type of wish list. As a child, you may have made up a list for Santa Claus. I found with my own children that if I allowed them to look at Christmas catalogs or newspaper ads, their lists for Santa got longer and longer—even when they knew that it was Mom and Dad who were providing the goodies. Our prayers are not meant to be wish lists for God to fill. Yes, we may ask for things we need, and even for things we want, but I feel that there should be a higher purpose for our asking than just "gimme, gimme, gimme." I have looked at examples of prayer in Scripture, and I did not find one example where a person prayed for a new tent, a new robe, or a new camel. I have concluded therefore that these things are not supposed to be all that important. In fact, Jesus even tells us specifically not to worry about these things. (Matthew 6:25)

Second, true prayer is not a repetition of memorized phrases. (Matthew 6:7). We are to enter into prayer with our minds as well as our words (1 Corinthians 14:1). Prayer is personal; you are talking and someone else is listening. That someone else just happens to be God.

Third, to pray "in Jesus name" does not mean that we should tack that phrase onto the end of our prayers as a kind of magic spell. In the tale of Aladdin, one had to say the phrase "Open Sesame" to unlock the door to the treasure cave. "In Jesus name" is not the spell to unlock the treasures of heaven. God is not bound to give us everything we ask for. He is not a cosmic Santa Claus or a genie in a bottle; there are no magic words to make Him respond. God will give us some of the things we ask for because He wants to bless us. He will give us some things we haven't even thought to ask for. He will also not give us some of the things we want.

Does that mean He doesn't care about us, or that He is too busy to be bothered with us? Of course not. Would you give a child everything he asked for? Some parents do, and they end up with spoiled, selfish children. Sometimes they end up with extremely dysfunctional families as well. God knows what we can handle and what will be the best for us. If He does not give us a specific blessing, there is a very good reason.

So if prayer is not a wish list, a magic spell, or repetition of well-worn phrases, then what is it? If I am not supposed to ask for all the things I want, what am I supposed to pray for? How am I supposed to talk to God? Let's back up a minute to that phrase "in Jesus name." I have said that these are not "magic words." I have not said what I believe the phrase really means. As I have been praying about this lesson, I have come to believe that this phrase directs us to think of all of life from Jesus' point of view. If we look at our lives from His perspective, we will see our blessings and our needs more clearly. We will be able to distinguish easily between needs and wants. We will be more thankful for the things we have and less envious of the things that others have. If we look at our lives through the eyes of Christ, we will be more sensitive to the needs of others. We will truly care about others, just as He does. We will want what is really best for them and for us, and we will trust Him to decide what that will be. We will be willing to relinquish control to Christ.

Actually, I think this is what the term *sanctification* means. I have been told that it means becoming more and more like Christ. Would it not also follow that as we become more like Christ, we would see things as He sees them? Those things that seem so important to us would become less important and the things we desire would correspond more and more to what He desires for us. As we see the world through the eyes of Christ, we won't want to make a wish list. We won't want most of that stuff anyway; we will see how foolish it all is.

So how do we pray? Ordinarily, our prayers should begin with praise. Think about who God is and what He has done. What specifically can you praise Him for? Let this be different each time you pray—today, at this very moment, what stands out to you that you want to praise God for? Think of all the attributes of God. Which are particularly relevant to you today?

Second, we should thank God for what He has done specifically for us. If you were to make a list of everything you could think of for which you could thank God, you should have a really long list. It isn't necessary to go through the whole list in every prayer. Focus on the things that you are really thankful for today.

Then third, we should confess our sins. God has said that He will forgive us for our sins and cast them as far away as the east is from the west. If we confess, we can have the blessing of knowing that our sins are forgiven. And once a sin has been confessed and forgiven, let it go.

Finally, we can pray for ourselves and others. In this, we should try to see our lives and the lives of those around us as Christ sees us. We should not ask for things that we know are against His will, or things that we know will tempt us to sin or cause us to struggle in our Christian lives.

We can be honest with God about our disappointments, our frustrations, and our unmet longings. The Psalms give us examples of all kinds of things said to God in prayer. In Psalm 18:46, the psalmist is praising God; in Psalm 22:2, he is crying out to God because of unanswered prayer; in Psalm 38:18, he is confessing his sins; in Psalm 71:20, he is making a statement; in Psalm 13:1, he is asking a question. We should talk to God in an immediate and personal way; you may speak to God as you would a friend, or your language may be more formal. It doesn't matter, as long as you give God the respect and worship He is due. Nothing is hidden from God anyway, so we might as well talk to Him about it all.

But let's keep it fresh. Beware of repeating the same thing over and over. Imagine you have a friend who calls you at 7:30 and says, "Hello _____. I am so glad you are my friend. You are a wonderful, caring, and loving person. You have helped me so many times in the past. I am grateful that you are my friend. I would like to ask you to continue to help me in my need, and I will be truly grateful." Then she hangs up. You are a little shocked, but the call has made you feel good. The next day, at 7:30, she calls again, and says, "Hello _____. I am so glad you are my friend. You are a wonderful, caring, and loving person. You have helped me so many times in the past. I am grateful that you are my friend. I would like to ask you to continue to help me in my need, and I will be truly grateful." This time you are not as shocked, but you don't feel as good about it as you did yesterday. The third day, you are kind of expecting the call, and sure enough, at 7:30 the phone rings. The voice at the other end says, "Hello _____. I am so glad you are my friend. You are a wonderful, caring, and loving person. You have helped me so many times in the past. I am grateful that you are my friend. I would like to ask you to continue to help me in my need, and I will be truly grateful."

Aren't you ready to ask this caller, who really means well, "Can't you think of anything else to say?! I appreciate what you are trying to do, but can't we have a conversation? Can't you be more specific about what is going on in your life? Can't I talk to you?"

Which brings up an element of communication that I didn't mention earlier—the feedback. The receiver of the communication can send a message back to the source. Take time to be quiet and listen to what God may be telling you. Read His Word. Hear what God has to say to you.

One of the best promises that God gives us is that if we don't know how to pray in a certain situation or if we pray for the wrong thing, the Holy Spirit will take our prayers and present them to God the Father as they should be. He will pray for us in a way that goes beyond our words. Not only can we pray to God, but we can give our problems to Him and ask Him to pray for us! We don't have to know what to ask for.

God also promises that He will hear and answer our prayers. He tells us in His Word that the prayer of a righteous person is powerful and effective. So who are the righteous? According to God, that would be everyone who has been saved by Christ. When we receive Christ as our Savior, not only are our sins forgiven, but the righteous life that Jesus lived is credited to us. It is as though we ourselves lived a perfectly righteous life. So all who trust in Christ are the righteous ones, the ones whose prayers are powerful and effective.

Do you believe that? When you pray, do you believe that there is power in your prayers? Do you expect God to act? If not, are you praying selfishly, looking at the world through your own eyes and not through the eyes of Christ? Let that be the thing you pray for—to see with the eyes of Christ.

8

LESSON 8
"OUR FATHER WHO IS IN HEAVEN"

Question 99: What rule has God given for our direction in prayer?

Answer: The whole Word of God is of use to direct us in prayer, but the special rule of direction is the form of prayer that Christ taught His disciples, commonly called "the Lord's Prayer.

1. Where was Jesus when he taught the disciples "the Lord's Prayer"?
   Read Matthew 4:23-25

2. When was this instruction repeated?
   Read Luke 11:1-4

3. Do you think that repeating the Lord's Prayer over and over mindlessly is an acceptable form of prayer?
   Read Matthew 6:7

4. How are we to pray the Lord's Prayer (or any other prayer)?
   Read 1 Corinthians 14:15

Question 100: What does the preface of the Lord's Prayer teach us?

Answer: The preface of the Lord's Prayer, which is, "Our Father in heaven," teaches us to draw near to God with all holy reverence and confidence, as children to a father, able and ready to help us; and that we should pray with and for others.

5. How does a person become a child of God?
   Read John 1:12

6. Why were the Pharisees so angry with Jesus?
   Read Mark 14:60-64

7. According to the Bible, who are Jesus' brothers and sisters?
   Read Matthew 12:50

8. According to Scripture, who is our brother?
   Read Philemon 1:8-16; 1 Corinthians 7:12; 1 Corinthians 5:11

9. How are we to treat those who are not our brothers?
   Read Matthew 5:44; Romans 12:20

LESSON 8
"OUR FATHER WHO IS IN HEAVEN"

Catechism Questions 99 and 100

HOW OFTEN DO YOU PRAY THE LORD'S PRAYER? OR, MORE IMPOR-
tantly, *how* do you pray the Lord's Prayer? Jesus gave us this prayer in answer
to his disciples' request to teach them to pray. According to most Bible scholars,
it is meant as a guide for prayer, not as a prayer to be repeated over and over
without thinking about its meaning. We know that Jesus did not intend this as
merely a rote or repetitive prayer because he tells us in the book of Matthew not
to keep babbling like pagans, who think their prayers will be heard because
of their many words. Paul tells us in 1 Corinthians that we should pray with
our minds.

Does this mean that we should not repeat the Lord's Prayer as part of a
church worship service? I don't think so, but it does mean that we should
focus our minds on what we are praying. Whether we are praying the Lord's
Prayer or any other prayer, our minds should be totally engaged.

It stands to reason, then, that we need to know what the words of the
Lord's Prayer really mean. Whether we use this prayer as a prayer by itself or
as a guide to how we should form other prayers, Jesus gave us this example
in answer to the disciples' question about how we should pray. If we are
going to understand it as we pray it, or understand how it should guide our
prayers, we need to be clear about what it is really saying.

So let's start with the first phrase, "Our Father in Heaven" (or "Our Father
who is in Heaven"). Did you know that in the entire Old Testament, not once
does anyone call God his father? God is called *the* Father, but not *my* Father.
To have called God your Father would have meant that you considered
yourself equal with God. Think about earthly fathers. Have you ever heard
of anyone who escaped trouble with authorities because of who his or her
father was? Of course you have. Even in society today, we are sometimes
identified by who our father is or was. To call someone like Donald Trump
or Ronald Reagan your father implies a relationship that most people do not

have with these men and would almost automatically cause a person to be treated differently.

This is the kind of relationship that Jesus claimed to have with His Father and that He in turn gave to us with our Father.

This is why the Pharisees were so angry with Jesus' teaching. Of course they were offended when he called them a brood of vipers and a whited sepulcher. But the worst offense was that He claimed to be equal with God; He called God His Father and said that He was one with the Father. According to Jewish law, this was a crime worthy of death—unless, of course, it was the truth.

Christians today are so accustomed to using the term "Father" to refer to God that we don't give it a second thought. Most of our prayers begin with the term. We may add descriptors such as "Our heavenly Father" or "Almighty Father," but the concept is almost always there. We have numerous hymns which also reinforce the idea that we are God's children. So we lose sight of how awesome that really is.

Before I accepted the Lord Jesus as my Savior and turned my life over to Him, I had a strong sense of obligation to God. I knew there was a God. I knew Jesus was His Son. And I was determined to do what I could to please Him (at least some of the time). I read my Bible every night, went to church every Sunday, and tried not to cuss. I was almost superstitious about doing these things; I did not want to offend God.

When I began attending a college Sunday School class, I realized that the other students in the class had a different relationship with God than I had, and I wanted it, too. I scheduled an appointment with the pastor and asked him, "How do I get the kind of relationship with God that those other students have?" (Wouldn't you love to be asked that kind of question?!) He explained God's plan of salvation, and I immediately prayed to receive Christ.

I remember walking to class the next day with a feeling of complete awe. As I looked at the world around me, I knew that the God who had created it all loved me personally. He had chosen me to be His child. I was a child of the King of the Universe! To this day I continue to be awed by that knowledge. If you have been a Christian for a while, reflect on who you are before God. He loves you, each of you, individually and personally. You are not just part of a vast population of humans—you are unique and special to God. And this relationship does not apply to everyone.

In the nineteenth century, according to R. C. Sproul,[9] a philosopher named Adolf von Harnack developed a view of religion that had two concepts at its core: the universal fatherhood of God and the universal brotherhood of man. You have probably heard those concepts expressed in one form or another. But are they true? And how do they affect the way we see ourselves before God?

If God is a universal Father, then He is the father of everyone in the same manner. Think of an earthly father. He may have several children with different mothers, but he is equally the father of all of them. If he were to single out one or two of his children for special favors, we would condemn him for his unequal treatment of his children. We would feel that all of his children belong to him and deserve an equal share of his love and attention.

Now think of a potter with a vast collection of pottery that he has created. Suppose he decides to put one of his pots on the coffee table in his living room and he uses another pot outside to hold the potting soil for his garden. He is treating those pots very differently, but would we condemn him for that? Would we insist that he must treat all of his creations equally? Of course not. He made the pots and he can decide how they are to be used.

So which one of the examples above is a better picture of God? Although many of us would prefer it to be the example of the father, that is not the picture that the Bible gives us. According to Romans 9, God has created us just as a potter creates a clay pot. He owns us because He has created us. And since we belong to Him, it is His decision how we are to be treated.

Now suppose that the potter is miraculously able to breathe life into his pots, and he chooses to do so. He selects certain pots, gives them life, and adopts them as his children. Think of the story of Pinocchio. He was a puppet, not a pot, but the idea is pretty much the same. Is the potter obligated to breathe life into all the pots? Not at all. He created them, they belong to him, and he can use them however he wants.

That is the picture of God. He has created us, He owns us, and He gives eternal life to whomever He chooses. Those are the people who are His children. We are given life and adopted by Him. He is the only one who can give us the right, or even the power, to become His children.

Now, back to the pots. How should those pots who have been brought to life behave? Should they look down on the other pots and misuse or abuse them? No, because all of the pots are the work of the potter. They should all be treated with dignity because they are all his creations. If the living pots love the potter, then they will take care of what he has made. Should the living pots feel pride that they have been given life? I wouldn't think so. Instead they should feel supremely grateful that they are alive.

So what about the "universal brotherhood of man"? Is everyone your brother or sister? Contrary to what you may have been taught, the answer is no. Although every human being is a creation of God, all human beings are not children of God. In both the Old and New Testaments, the term "brother" has one of two meanings. First, the word can refer to a sibling, the son of your father, mother, or both. Second, the word can refer to someone who shares your belief in God. Those who are outside the family of faith are referred to as friends, neighbors, or even enemies, but never as brothers. God also gives us instructions about how we are to treat people who are outside the faith, and we are always told to be kind to them. But there are special instructions about how we are to treat our "brothers."

If we have been adopted by God, we should not be proud of that fact, but humbly grateful for the incredible gift of life and sonship. We should give others who are also His children special consideration. And because everyone is a creation of God, and thus our neighbor, we should treat everyone we know with dignity and respect.

9

LESSON 9
PRAYING TO HONOR GOD

Question 101: For what do we pray in the first petition?

Answer: In the first petition, which is, "Hallowed be your name," we pray that God would enable us, and others, to glorify Him in all the means by which he makes Himself known, and that he would arrange all things to His own glory.

1. What does the word "hallowed" mean?
    Read Exodus 20:11 in the King James Version, then in a more modern translation.

2. What does the word "holy" mean?
    Read Isaiah 5:16; Ephesians 5:27

3. God is holy. What other things does He call holy?
    Read Genesis 2:3; Leviticus 27:21, 30; Numbers 18:19; Isaiah 56:7

4. How does God describe His people in Rome and Corinth?
   Read Romans 1:7; 1 Corinthians 1:2

5. Were the Christians in Rome and Corinth completely righteous and blameless?
   Read Romans 14:10; 1 Corinthians 3:3

6. Why were these people considered to be holy?
   Read Leviticus 20:26; Deuteronomy 7:6; 1 Peter 2:9

7. How do we keep the name of God holy?
   Read Isaiah 29:23; Ezekiel 20:39; Exodus 20:7

Question 102: For what do we pray in the second petition?

Answer: In the second petition, which is, "Your kingdom come," we pray that Satan's kingdom may be destroyed, and that the kingdom of grace may be advanced, ourselves and others brought into it, and kept in it, and that the kingdom of glory may be hastened.

8. Where is the kingdom of God?
   Read John 18:36

62

9. What are characteristics of those who are living in the kingdom of God?

   Read Romans 14:17

10. How do we enter the kingdom of God?

    Read John 3:3

LESSON 9
PRAYING TO HONOR GOD

Catechism Questions 101 and 102

MY GRANDFATHER WAS ADAMANT ABOUT PROTECTING THE NAME OF God. Nothing made him more angry than for someone to misuse God's name. On one occasion, my mother was driving him somewhere, and when they got out of the car, she accidentally slammed the car door on his hand. In her moment of distress, she said, "Oh my God!" With his hand still stuck in the door, my grandfather berated her for misusing God's name. He was more concerned with honoring God than with the pain he was obviously in.

And he was right. We must be careful not to use God's name when we are not specifically referring to Him. But there is much more involved in hallowing God's name; we must revere and honor all things having to do with God. And we must center our lives around giving Him all the glory.

I am in the middle of reading the book *Radical* by David Platt. Because I do not believe that anything happens by chance, I do not believe that it is by coincidence that the chapter I read last night concerned our duty to extend the glory of God. God knew I would be writing this today, and He wanted me to expand my understanding of what it means to glorify Him. Please indulge me as I tell you a couple of things Platt says in his book.

First, Platt says[10] that we were all created for two purposes: to enjoy God's grace and to extend His glory. (Sound familiar? If not, look at Catechism Question 1, in the book *Created by God—Purchased by Christ.*) If we bother to think about God's grace at all, we are usually pretty good at enjoying it. It is not hard to be thankful for God's saving us and His providing for all of our needs. So that is not where Platt places his emphasis.

What does it mean to extend the glory of God and how do we do it? Platt refers to several Old Testament stories (Abraham; the Israelites crossing the Red Sea; Shadrach, Meshach, and Abednego; and Daniel. As he reminds us, the end result in each of these stories was that others besides the main characters began to glorify God. God blessed the men in these stories, but in doing so, He extended His glory to come from others.

Second, Platt begins to hit where it hurts. He asks what the gospel is all about. What is your answer? In your answer, is the word "me" or "I" in there somewhere? Is the gospel that Christ died for *me*? Or that God gave His Son so *I* could have eternal life? That is only a small part of the correct answer. The gospel is that the triune God determined that God the Son would come to earth, live a sinless life, die a cruel death, and be raised from the dead to save those whom the Father had given Him and who would believe in Him so that He might be glorified.

Do you see the difference? In the first two answers, the focus of the gospel is on me; in the last, the focus is on God. Where should the focus be? Does God bless me so that I can have a comfortable life? Does God design churches so I can be at ease as I attempt to worship Him? What does God want for my life—for me to be happy or for me to glorify Him? Or perhaps, does He want me to glorify Him so I can be truly and deeply joyful in His kingdom?

God's Kingdom is not of this world. When we pray for His kingdom to come, we are praying for one of two things. First, we could be praying for Christ to return and take us to His heavenly kingdom. Or second, we could be praying for Christ to enlarge His kingdom here on earth. I have decided to focus on the second option. How does Christ enlarge His kingdom here on earth? He could do it any way He wanted to, but in His infinite wisdom, He has decided to use people.

Look at Matthew 28:19—"Go therefore and make disciples of all nations, baptizing them in the name of the Father and of the Son and of the Holy Spirit, teaching them to observe all that I have commanded you." Is this a request, an invitation, or a command? Does Jesus tell us, "It would be really great if you would go into all the world and teach others about me"? Does He say, "Everyone is invited to participate in the sharing of the good news of the gospel with the rest of the world"? Does He say, "If you are called to do so, go into all the world and share the gospel"? Or does He simply tell us, "Go"?

What if we don't feel "called" to go? Then we should get over it, because we are all called. When we become part of the kingdom of God, we are called to go and tell others. If you have confessed your sins and yielded control of your life to Jesus (and that's what being born again means), then your primary purpose in God's kingdom is to spread the news—wherever God puts you. "Going" does not necessarily involve leaving your home town; there are plenty of people who need the gospel who live all around you. But "going" might involve a move. Would you be willing to do that?

I was at a church missions conference many years ago, and at the end of one sermon, the preacher asked us to stand if we were willing to serve God wherever He would lead us to go. Only a handful of people stood up. I was horrified. The preacher was not asking us to volunteer to go to Outer Mongolia or the inner city, he was just asking if we were willing to do what God wanted us to do! At least two hundred people in that congregation smugly sat there telling God, "Not me, buster. I'm staying right here."

So let me ask you. Are you willing? Will you do whatever God asks of you? Will you go wherever He sends you? He may want to keep you right where you are and have you extend His glory to those around you; but He might want to uproot you from where you have grown comfortable and complacent and plant you in a place where you can be of more service to Him. It's really not about us; it's all about Him.

Please don't say that missions is not your gift. It's not on the gift list. Everyone is commanded to serve God using the particular gifts God has given them. That's what missions is. My definition of missions is to extend the good news of Christ and the love of Christ to those who do not believe. It doesn't matter if they are on the other side of the world or live next door. There are so many types of missions. If our gift is mercy, we can serve the poor; if our gift is hospitality, we can house the homeless; if our gift is teaching, we can teach the prisoners, the children, and all those who need the gospel; if our gift is encouraging, we can lift up those who are troubled and discouraged.

Many people use the excuse that they don't want to go overseas because they are concerned about the needs here at home. But are they truly serving God to help meet those needs? Do they volunteer at homeless shelters? Do they visit prisons? Do they help women with unplanned pregnancies? Do they assist victims of domestic abuse? Do they build homes for those who need them? Do they visit the sick (those they don't know)? There are lots of ways to glorify God. What are you doing?

Maybe you are thinking that you are doing some of those things, but you are using your gifts to serve the church. Of course we can use our gifts within the church; God wants us to do that. Churches are made up of people with needs and problems, and they need our help. But nowhere in Scripture does God tell us to limit the use of our gifts to the church. Certainly, we should glorify God by serving Him in the church, but let's not stop there. The Great Commission calls us to spread the Gospel, not just maintain it.

And while we're on the subject, are you concerned about getting credit for what you do in the church? If someone in your church made a list of people who have served in your church, would you be upset if your name wasn't on it? I think all of us are still sinful enough that we would resent that. But who is supposed to get the glory for the things done in God's name? Us or God? If our service is done to glorify ourselves, then maybe that's not the kind of service God wants.

God moves some people to places other than where they were born. He wants those people to serve him there. We call those people missionaries. Why? They are doing the same thing we are all supposed to be doing, they are just doing it in a new and different place. That doesn't excuse the rest of us for not doing anything. We each have gifts; if God has left us where we are, then He expects us to use those gifts where we are. What are you doing with your gift to help those both inside and outside the church body? Where do you think God wants to use you?

10

LESSON 10
PRAYING FOR GOD'S WILL
AND OUR OWN NEEDS

Question 103: For what do we pray in the third petition?

Answer: In the third petition, which is, "Your will be done, on earth as it is in heaven," we pray that God, by His grace, would make us able and willing to know, obey, and submit to His will in all things, as the angels do in heaven.

1. What is God's will for us?
    Read 1 Thessalonians 4:3-6; 5:16-18

2. What else is God's will for us?
    Read 1 Peter 2:13-15; 3:17

3. What were we created for?
    Read Ephesians 2:10

4. What have we been predestined for?
    Read Romans 8:28-29

Question 104: For what do we pray in the fourth petition?

Answer: In the fourth petition, which is, "Give us this day our daily bread," we pray that, of God's free gift, we may receive a sufficient portion of good things of this life, and enjoy His blessing with them.

5. What things do we need physically?
    Read Matthew 6:31-32; Matthew 9:12; Psalm 142:6

6. How much do we need?
    Read Exodus 16:18; Proverbs 30:8-9

7. What things do we need spiritually?
    Read Luke 10:38-42; Acts 3:19; 1 Corinthians 12:21

LESSON 10
PRAYING FOR GOD'S WILL
AND OUR OWN NEEDS

Catechism Questions 103 and 104

ONE THING I HAVE NOTICED AS I HAVE BEEN WRITING THESE BIBLE
studies is that the more I deal with the doctrines of our faith, the more I realize how far I fall short of what God expects of me. This lesson has affected me
greatly in this way. So as you read this study, please be aware that this one was
written to me, and I pray that you will be convicted as I have been.

To begin, in the third petition of the Lord's Prayer, we pray for God's
will to be done on earth. What exactly does that mean? And do we really,
honestly, want that?

Let's look at what the Bible tells us about God's will for us. First, God's
will is that we should be sanctified and conformed to the image of His Son,
Jesus Christ. This requires that we live in a certain way. We should avoid
sexual immorality and control our own bodies, and we should not wrong or
take advantage of our brothers. We should be joyful always, pray continually,
and give thanks in all circumstances. (*All* circumstances, not just the ones
we like.) We are to submit to all earthy authorities and do good works to
silence our critics. And finally, sometimes it is God's will for us to suffer for
the sake of Christ.

Is this what you think about when you pray for God's will to be done? Are
you really asking for God's will to prevail, or are you asking that God put His
rubber stamp on *your* will? Are you thinking only of the "positive" aspects
of God's will—that all men serve and love Him? Have you ever considered
that God's will might mean your suffering for Him? That God might want
you to change some of your behavior, or even your thoughts? Are there times
when you have been opposed to your earthly authorities and said something
like, "He's not *my* President!" But he is (or she is), no matter who holds that
office. He is your President because he has been elected by the people of

the country; but more importantly, he is your President because God has put him in that position. Are you fighting God's will in this regard?

Are you joyful always? Of course we are all joyful at times, but I'm afraid that in my case that usually occurs when I get something I want or when everything's going my way. I am not usually joyful when I am suffering or especially when my children are suffering. I am not joyful when I hear dire predictions about the future of my country or its economy. I am not joyful when I have to do things I really don't want to do.

But I should be. God's will for me is to be joyful at all times, and He also wants me to be thankful in all circumstances. I must be thankful when God showers His blessings on me, and I must be thankful when He teaches me the lessons I need to learn. Those lessons are often not a lot of fun. They can be painful and require a lot of hard work and soul-searching. But I must be thankful. I must be thankful when I have plenty; and I must be thankful when I don't. I must be thankful when my friends support and encourage me; and I must be thankful when they criticize or neglect me. God tells us to be thankful in everything.

In the Lord's Prayer, we pray that God's will be done on earth as it is in Heaven; that is, that God's will be done perfectly. In Heaven, there is no sin; all of the angels and the saints who have been taken to be with the Lord are in perfect obedience to Him. Is that what you want for your life? To be in perfect obedience? What would you have to give up or change in order to accomplish that goal? Is that what you are praying for?

Not only do we pray for God's will to be done, which is honestly a little frightening, but the next thing we pray is that God would provide for our needs. "Give us this day our daily bread" asks God to give us what we need for each day, on a daily basis. There are two things to consider as we think about this petition: what our needs are, and the daily provision of those needs.

According to Scripture, what do we *need*? Using a complete concordance, I was able to find eight things that God says we need: food, drink, clothing, medical care, rescue from our enemies, repentance, Jesus' teaching, and fellowship with other believers. That's all. Is that enough?

I like to watch TV shows about home makeovers and home buying and selling. I really don't know why I like those, but I do. Lately I have been paying more attention to the reasons the people are remodeling their homes or buying new ones. Most of them say that they need a more modern home or they need more space. Really? One couple with two children, living in a 2,000 square foot home, were desperate for more space. Think about that for a minute. They were saying that 500 square feet each is not enough.

In 1862, Congress passed the Homestead Act, giving pioneers the opportunity to obtain land by living on the land, growing crops, and building a 12 x 14 foot home. That is 168 square feet. For an entire family. Yet the family on that TV show couldn't live in a home where each person in the home had almost three times that much space! And we don't even need to go to the past for such figures. The average Habitat for Humanity home built in Kenya today has 365 square feet. The average house in Sweden has 1,291 square feet. The average house in the United States has 2,330 square feet.

Think about your own life. Do you have food, drink, clothing, and medical care? Are you being pursued by enemies? (Real enemies, not just disagreeable people.) Have you repented of your sins? Do you have a Bible? Do you have fellowship with other believers? If you have these things, then you have what you need. Anything else that you have is just gravy. All of the other things that you think you couldn't live without are blessings—good gifts that God has given you. How much paper would you need to make a list of every single thing that you have that does not fit into the list above?

When you pray, do you pray as though you need those extra things? Or are you honest in admitting that they are things you want? I personally think it's okay to ask God for what we want; He promises to give us the desires of our heart. But we don't need to fool ourselves. Most of what we want is just that—a want. And I am as guilty, or perhaps more guilty, of that than anyone else.

Okay, so if we will admit it, we don't need nearly as much as we have. We are supremely blessed. That's not all we are asking in the fourth petition of the Lord's Prayer. We are also asking that we be given what we need on a daily basis.

Remember the Israelites as they wandered in the desert. They were given manna every morning, but it didn't last until the next day (except on the Sabbath). They were only given enough for the day.

We are not in the habit of living from day to day. We stock up food for the week, month, or even year. We are able to do that because we have technology available that will preserve the food for us. But we need to recognize that God is still providing for us day by day. The technology could fail, a natural disaster could hit, and we could lose it all.

And it's not just food. Are you stocking up money to provide for yourself in the future? There is nothing wrong with saving; in fact, I encourage it. But how much is enough? Are you failing to give to the Lord or to the needy because you are hoarding money for your own future? God tells us to give to the needy and trust Him to provide for our needs. Remember that your bank account, your job, your retirement benefits, etc. all ultimately come from the Lord—not from the government, your employer, or your 401K.

When we pray for our needs, let's make sure they really are needs. If they are wants, then let's at least be honest enough to admit it. Let us all be willing to live according to God's will and to let Him provide for us. God loved you enough to sacrifice His own Son so that you could be with Him forever. Do you think He won't provide for you now?

11

LESSON 11
PRAYING FOR
FORGIVENESS AND DELIVERANCE

Question 105: For what do we pray in the fifth petition?

Answer: In the fifth petition, which is, "Forgive us our debts, as we also have forgiven our debtors," we pray that God, for Christ's sake, would freely pardon all our sins, which we are more encouraged to ask because by His grace we are enabled from the heart to forgive others.

1. How extensive is God's forgiveness?
   Read Jeremiah 31:34; Psalm 103:12

2. How does God describe His forgiveness of sins?
   Read Isaiah 1:18

3. What did Jesus say about our forgiving other people?
   Read Matthew 6:14-15

4. How did Paul describe a mature Christian?
    Read Ephesians 4:14-15

5. What is the situation for anyone who causes a young believer to sin?
    Read Matthew 18:6

6. What did Jesus say about people who cause others to sin?
    Read Luke 17:1

7. How are we to use the gifts God has given us?
    Read 1 Peter 4:10

8. How are we to treat those who have fallen into sin?
    Read Galatians 6:1

Question 106: For what do we pray in the sixth petition?

Answer: In the sixth petition, which is, "And lead us not into temptation, but deliver us from evil," we pray that God would either keep us from being tempted to sin, or support and deliver us when we are tempted.

9. What does God promise when we are tempted to sin?
   Read 1 Corinthians 10:13

10. Why is Christ able to help us endure temptation?
    Read Hebrews 4:15

11. Who is it that tempts us to sin?
    Read 1 Thessalonians 3:5; James 1:13-14

LESSON 11
PRAYING FOR
FORGIVENESS AND DELIVERANCE

Catechism Questions 105 and 106

I AM PRETTY GOOD AT DOING LAUNDRY NOW, BUT THAT HASN'T ALWAYS been the case. When my husband and I were newly married, I washed a load of clothes that included all types of fabrics and colors. As I took the clothes out of the dryer, I realized that all of his white shirts were now a blotchy pale pink. There was no way he could wear them. So I tried to get the color out. I ended up using a color-remover and boiling them on the stove, which really stunk up the house. And those shirts were never 100% white again.

Our sins are not a pale pink; they are bright blood red. Think of them as blood-stained clothes. But God can remove every hint of stain and make us white as snow. That is how He describes His forgiveness. He also tells us that He will take our sins and separate them from us as far as infinity and that He will not remember them. That means that when we pray, we must remember how our Father forgives us, and then forgive those whom we need to forgive. We must pray as a forgiven sinner who forgives others. So let's talk about forgiveness. What does it mean to forgive? In the study at the beginning of this lesson, I asked a lot of questions about this phrase, and you may have wondered where I was going. I want us to truly understand what forgiveness is and what it isn't.

We know that when someone wrongs us, we are supposed to forgive them. Does that mean that we are to cast their sins away and remember them no more? Jesus told Peter that we are to forgive our brother the same offense seventy-seven times (or seventy times seven). Does that mean that on that seventy-eighth (or four hundred ninety-first) offense, we can hold as much of a grudge as we want to? Does it mean that we must continue to allow someone to sin against us?

Let's apply a hypothetical example. Susan has a brother Larry, who is a drug addict. Larry has borrowed money from Susan on several occasions, only to use it to pay for his habit. He has been evicted from his home three times, and each time Susan has let him stay with her. Each time he has stolen items from her home to pawn, again to feed his habit. What does the Bible say about Susan's forgiveness of Larry?

First, the Bible says she must forgive. Does that mean she must promise never to remember what he has done? As my pastor, John Reeves, pointed out to me, that is an impossible promise. We do not have that kind of control over our memories. When the Bible says that God does not remember our sins, it does not mean that He has a cosmic memory lapse. He knows what we have done and He will always know it. It does mean that He will not dwell on it or bring it up to us ever again. That is something that we can promise.

Now back to Susan and her dilemma. She can promise never to bring up Larry's sins again. Does that mean that she must continue to "loan" him money and to let him "crash" at her place? What else does the Bible have to say about how we treat others? Paul tells us that if a brother is caught in sin, we are to restore him gently. That means that we are to lovingly confront the sinner about his/her sin. So Susan needs to confront Larry about his actions.

Some people's interpretation of the concept of forgiveness is that when you forgive, you are in effect saying, "It's all right. It doesn't matter. It's no big deal." Think of forgiveness from God's perspective. Do we really think that when God forgives our sin, He is telling us that it's all right—it's no big deal? Of course not. Our sins are a huge deal. Jesus Christ lowered Himself to take on human flesh and to be tortured and crucified because that was the price of our forgiveness. Forgiveness does not mean that the offense is not important. It means that we will not continue to dwell on the offense.

We are also told that we should never be the cause of someone else's sin. The psychological word for this is "enabling." An enabler is a person who helps, or enables, another to continue a negative behavior, or a sin. For Susan to continue to provide Larry with money, or even a place to stay, she would be acting as his enabler. She would be assisting him in his sinfulness.

Susan is also told to be a faithful steward of what God has given her. To allow her gifts from God to be used to further Larry's sin would be dishonoring to God. She is also told in Ephesians that a mature Christian is not misled by the cunning and craftiness of deceivers. I have had quite a bit of experience with addictive personalities, and I can attest to the fact that there are probably no more deceitful, cunning, and crafty people on the planet.

So my conclusion is that forgiveness does not mean that we are to be doormats, or enablers. Forgiveness is largely for our own benefit. Grudges can be very heavy things to carry around; forgiveness transfers that weight to Christ. There is amazing freedom in forgiveness.

To those of you who are dealing with an addict, an alcoholic, an adulterer, or anyone else caught up in sin, I want to admonish you to stop enabling. It can be painful to stop, but it can be more painful not to. Please remember that no one will stop his sinful, selfish behavior unless he decides to stop. Nothing you can say or do will make him or her change. It's like talking to air. Say what you have to say once or twice, then allow the addict, etc., in your life to live with the consequences of his own actions. Live your own life. Separate yourself from him if you need to do that for your own mental health. I've been there and I know what you are going through. It will be hard, but you will be better in the long run.

It is interesting that when Paul tells us to restore those who are sinful, he also tells us to take care that we are not tempted. I have always understood that to mean that we should be careful that we do not begin to indulge in the same sinful lifestyle. Perhaps he also meant that we should not fall into the sin of enabling. Regardless of his meaning, though, we are to pray that we would not fall into temptation.

Where does temptation come from? Only two sources—the devil and our own desires. But how does the devil tempt us? Does he bring up things we never even wanted to do and try to tempt us to do them? He is much smarter than that. Satan and his legions are very observant of those who follow Christ. They know what sins we have committed in the past, and which ones are the hardest for us to resist. Those are the sins they will tempt us with.

So really, it's just us. Our own desires are where the temptations come from. Whether we are encouraged by the evil one, or just by our own thoughts and feelings, we ourselves are to blame. Do you remember the comedian Flip Wilson? He had a variety show in the 1970's on which he played a number of characters. His most famous was a woman named Geraldine, whose most famous line was, "The devil made me do it!" Flip Wilson was really funny, but this excuse is really not. The devil can't make us do anything. We do things because we want to do them. And even Geraldine knew that.

So what do we do when we find temptation almost impossible to bear? When we really, really want to give in? We run as fast as we can to our Savior. He understands, because He endured every temptation that we will ever face. But He never succumbed; He resisted them all. So He can help us to resist. He knows exactly what you are going through, and he knows exactly how to beat it. Let him show you.

The problem is that much of the time, we don't really want to resist. We don't go to Jesus because we don't want His help. We want to use Geraldine's excuse. Give it up. Jesus knows better and so do you. Pray for the strength to fight temptation, and pray that you would not be tempted in the first place. Forgive others when they give in, but don't be the one who helps them continue to fall. Jesus told us to pray for these things because He promises to give them to those who ask.

12

LESSON 12
THE KINGDOM, THE POWER, AND THE GLORY

Question 107: What does the conclusion of the Lord's Prayer teach us?

Answer: The conclusion of the Lord's Prayer, which is, "For yours is the kingdom and the power and the glory, forever. Amen," teaches us to take our encouragement in prayer from God only, and in our prayers to praise Him, ascribing kingdom, power, and glory to Him, and in testimony of our desire and assurance to be heard, we say, "Amen."

1. To which people will God give His kingdom?
   Read Matthew 5:3, 10

2. Who will be called least and greatest in the kingdom of heaven?
   Read Matthew 5:19

3. Who will not enter the kingdom of heaven?
   Read Matthew 5:20

4. Who will enter the kingdom of heaven?
    Read Matthew 7:21

5. Where is the kingdom of God?
    Read John 18:36

6. How did Jesus show His power to those around Him?
    Read Luke 4:36, 6:19

7. What kind of power did Jesus give His disciples?
    Read Luke 9:1-3; 10:19

8. What kinds of things are under the power of Christ?
    Read John 13:3; Philippians 3:21

9. How was Pilate able to have power over Jesus?
    Read John 19:10-11

10. How did Paul describe the power of God?
    Read Ephesians 1:19-20

LESSON 12
THE KINGDOM, THE POWER,
AND THE GLORY

Catechism Question 107

WHERE IS YOUR HOME? MY ANSWER TO THAT WOULD DEPEND ON THE context. My current residence is in Mississippi; I have also lived in Oklahoma, California, Missouri, and South Dakota. But I consider Louisiana to be my home. However, none of those places is my real home. I am a citizen of Mississippi and of the United States, but more importantly, I am a citizen of the kingdom of God. My home, my real home, is in His kingdom.

So where is that exactly? In one sense, it's all around you. The kingdom of God is here on earth; the church is made up of its citizens. Have you ever met another American when in a foreign country? You instantly feel at home—here is someone from my home country. He or she will understand me and the way I think and behave.

Have you ever met a Christian in another country or city? You may dress differently and speak different languages, but there is a common bond and an uncommon affinity that draws you together. Again, he or she will understand how you think and behave—because again, you are citizens of the same kingdom.

God's Kingdom is not of this world, but it is in this world. We know we will enter His Kingdom when we die or when Jesus comes again. But we also live in the Kingdom now. Members of different cultures have different values and different ways of doing things. Have you noticed that the values of Christians are different from those who do not believe? Are there things that we do that others do not? There should be a difference. Our faith is to be lived out as we go through this life, because our culture is the culture of the Kingdom of God. We live here, but we are living in a foreign land. We can adapt to the culture of the country in which we live, but our true values and morals come from our "home country." And our home country will last forever. Nations come and go on earth. (If I ever manage to figure out all the countries in Africa, they change the next week!) But our Kingdom is here to stay because it is ruled and held together by the power of God Himself.

When we are confronted with the awe-inspiring majesty of creation, we become more truly aware of the power of God. Have you ever seen the Grand Canyon, the Rocky Mountains, or the Pacific Ocean? Were you awed by the splendor and power? We realize that there must be a powerful God to create such powerful scenery. How about a tornado, hurricane, tsunami, or other fierce storm? A friend of mine who is blind told me that he cannot see God's power in creation, but he can hear the thunder, and when he does, he feels the power of God.

Little children sing a song which goes, "My God is so big, so strong and so mighty, there's nothing that He cannot do." They have no doubts that God can do anything. But as adults we sometimes let the cares and worries of life overtake that knowledge. We seem to forget the power our God possesses. But remember the things Jesus did when He was on earth. He walked on water. Try that in your nearest puddle.

He told a storm to stop, and it stopped. The storm was so fierce that His disciples feared for their lives, but Jesus was sleeping. When they woke Him, He simply told the storm to stop. And it stopped instantly. Jesus fed thousands of people with five rolls and two fish. He healed people who had been sick, lame or blind for many years. He even raised people from the dead. Why do we doubt His power? Do we think that now that He is in Heaven, He has less power?! The majestic King of the Universe has lost His touch?!

But it's not Jesus alone who has power; He promised to give that power to us. Luke tells us that He gave power to the disciples to overcome all the power of the enemy. We know that Satan has power; the disciples were given more power. And we also have access to that same power. 2 Corinthians 10:3-4 tells us, "For though we live in the world, we do not wage war as the world does. The weapons we fight with are not the weapons of the world. On the contrary, they have divine power to demolish strongholds." In ourselves, we are powerless; but in God we have all the power of the Almighty because He works in us, through us, and beside us.

The kingdom and power belong to God alone, as does all the glory—forever. In a sense, God's power is manifested in His glory. Remember the story of Moses? He had been in close communion with God for forty days, and when he came down from the mountain, his face glowed with the reflected glory of God. It was so bright that he had to wear a veil or people could not bear to look at him. Imagine the brightest light you have ever seen. Now magnify that about a thousand times. Maybe that's close to the light of the glory of God. Remember that when Moses asked to see God, he was only allowed to see God's "back" because no one can live who sees the full unveiled glory of God. We are told in Revelation that the new earth will not need the sun, because the glory of God will provide our light forever.

Forever is a really long time. Think of what it means. We will live in perfect happiness, perfect unity, with no sadness, no hunger, no pain, no loneliness, forever. It will never stop. We will never be asked to give up the ones we love. There will be nothing that we need that is not provided. There will be no need to fear because there will be no sin. We will live in true joy—forever.

Suppose you were marooned on an island with a ship load of other people. Some of the people you like, but many you don't. There is a scarcity of resources, and some folks begin to hoard what they have, meaning that some people don't have enough. In an effort to survive, people begin to build shelters; some are hurt and even killed in the process. Fights break out. People steal from each other.

Then a small plastic raft lands on shore. The guy manning the raft tells you that he is there to take you to a ship that will take you home. The surf is rough and you will very likely be tossed around and get seasick, but you will eventually arrive at home. How would you feel? Would you be happy to see him? Would you get in that raft? Would you be excited to be going home?

That is exactly how we should feel about going to our eternal home. But many of us don't. Why not? We have willingly given our lives to Christ, but we don't want to go home. Maybe there is a fear of the unknown. But it is not really unknown; the best moments in our lives, those times that we want to remember and re-live over and over, are mere shadows of what our life will be when we go to our home that Jesus has prepared for us in His kingdom.

Our lives are meant to give glory to God. That is one of the two purposes for which we were created. Our chief end, our goal in life, our purpose, is to glorify God and enjoy Him forever. So it all fits together. Here we are, back at Catechism Question 1. Our lives can give God glory in His kingdom forever. God gives us His power to live those lives. We are His people, living in His kingdom. Let's enjoy Him.

END NOTES

1 "Grace." Dictionary.com. 2010.
2 "The Wit and Wisdom of Benjamin Franklin." *Saturday Evening Post.* p. 19. Nov/Dec 2007.
3 *Saturday Evening Post.*
4 Ron Kurtus. "Benjamin Franklin's Thirteen Virtues." School for Champions. 7 Feb. 2005. www.school-for-champions.com.
5 Benjamin Franklin. "Letter to Ezra Stiles." 9 March 1790, in John Bigelow, ed., *The Works of Benjamin Franklin*, at 12:185-86 (New York: Putnam's, 1904)
6 Joel B. Groat. "Bones, Stones, and the Scriptures: Has Archaeology Helped or Hurt the Bible?" Institute for Religious Research. 1992. www.irr.com.
7 Richard Pratt. *Pray With Your Eyes Open*. P & R. 1999
8 Manford G. Gutzke. *Plain Talk on Prayer*. Baker Book House. 1973.
9 R. C. Sproul. *The Prayer of the Lord*. Reformation Trust Publishing. 2009.
10 David Platt. *Radical*. Multnomah Books. 2010.